# Revolutionary Management

## John Adams on Leadership

Alan Axelrod, Ph.D.

The Lyons Press
Guilford, Connecticut
*An imprint of The Globe Pequot Press*

*For Anita and Ian*

The Lyons Press is an imprint of The Globe Pequot Press
Designed by Sheryl P. Kober
Library of Congress Cataloging-in-Publication Data is available on file.
ISBN 978-1-59921-411-5
Printed in the United States of America
10 9 8 7 6 5 4 3 2 1

# Contents

# *Managing Revolution*

⟶ IN 2007, THE UNITED STATES MINT
issued the first four "presidential $1 coins," featuring likenesses of
Washington, Jefferson, Madison—and John Adams. It was the first
American coin or currency to bear the image of our second president, a "founding father" who did make it onto a two-cent postage
stamp, but whose birthday has never been celebrated as a national
holiday and for whom very few public schools or similar institutions have been named. In contrast to Washington, Jefferson, the
non-presidential founding father Benjamin Franklin, and the latter-
day savior of the Union, Abraham Lincoln, John Adams has never
come to occupy an iconic niche in the American pantheon. Living
to his ninety-first year, Adams himself understood that "Mausole-
ums, statues, monuments will never be erected to me." He believed
that Americans would in due time mythologize the Revolution,
making of it "one continued lie from one end to the other. The essence of the whole will be that Dr. Franklin's electrical rod smote
the earth and out sprung General Washington. That Franklin elec-
trified him with his rod—and thence forward these two conducted
all the policy, negotiations, legislatures and war. These . . . lines con-
tain the whole fable, plot, and catastrophe." From this American
mythology Adams quite accurately believed he would be excluded.

A prime mover and key architect of American independence,
collaborator in the creation of America's first army—and the man
who nominated George Washington as that army's commander—as
well as founder and first champion of the U.S. Navy (stout "wooden
walls," he called ships, to defend America), John Adams negotiated

the foreign finance that made the Revolution possible, negotiated the treaties that ended it in absolute victory, opened the first U.S. embassy (in the Netherlands), and negotiated much-needed treaties of trade.

So, did the 2007 coin represent recognition long overdue? Not really. For the intention of the Mint is to commemorate every president—the likes of Washington, Lincoln, and the two Roosevelts, as well as that of Buchanan, Harding, and the two Bushes. For John Adams, as for the others, it was simply a matter of being present for the presidential roll call. He still failed to make the cut of those formative figures the mass of Americans consider "indispensable," to use the word biographer James Thomas Flexner applied to George Washington.

Why?

In the answer to this question is to be found the significance of John Adams not so much as the instigator or leader of the American Revolution, including its aftermath, but as its manager.

John Adams was an early opponent of the Stamp Act of 1765 and a charter advocate of the proposition Boston lawyer James Otis articulated in 1761, that taxation without representation is tyranny. Moreover, he was among the early minority of colonial political leaders willing to make the leap from that assertion to the proposition that, because the American colonies could never be adequately represented in Parliament, independence was the only real alternative to tyranny. Thus John Adams never had serious doubt about the necessity of independence—and yet, even as so many of his countrymen devoted themselves solely to tearing down British tyranny, Adams continually asked and endeavored to answer the question, *Then what?*

From the beginning, this set him apart. He opposed the royal tyranny of kings, but he opposed no less the hyper-democratic tyranny of the mob. Early in the revolutionary struggle, his wife, Abigail, quoted in a letter to him a line from Daniel Defoe: "Remember all men would be tyrants if they could." She was, of course, preaching to the choir. In sharp contrast to his great friend, sometime colleague, and sometime adversary, Thomas Jefferson, Adams believed that tyranny was the way of nature, including human nature. "Natural justice"? The phrase was for him a grotesque and tragic oxymoron. He never doubted the necessity of overthrowing the tyranny of George III, but he greatly feared replacing it with the tyranny of the mob, which was, as he saw it, humanity in a state of nature.

Revolution was needed. It was necessary to tear down tyranny, but Adams understood what many of his colleagues did not understand or, at least, refused to acknowledge. The tearing down was only half the necessary task—less than half, really. Far less. When a friend wrote to him about the sensation created by Thomas Paine's *Common Sense,* published on January 9, 1776, which largely galvanized the popular resolve for independence, Adams, who desperately wanted independence for America, nevertheless remarked to Abigail that Paine "has a better hand at pulling down than building."

To Senator Joseph Biden, Democrat of Delaware, President George W. Bush famously explained his approach to statesmanship early in 2004: "Joe, I don't do nuance." Nuance, in contrast, was precisely what John Adams did—and he did it lifelong, a fact that makes it so difficult for Americans to transform him into a one-dimensional icon. For neither fools nor icons do nuance.

Adams was resolute about the necessity of independence. He was outraged by the so-called "Olive Branch Petition" of Pennsylvania's John Dickinson, a fellow member of the Continental Congress, who sought an eleventh-hour reconciliation with the mother country. "Powder and artillery," Adams wrote in opposition to Dickinson, "are the most efficacious, sure and infallible conciliatory measures we can adopt," and he sent a letter to General Horatio Gates explaining that the "middle way is no way at all. . . . If we finally fail in this great and glorious contest, it will be by bewildering ourselves groping for the middle way." And yet Adams understood that independence alone was no answer to the question of *What next?* It was at most a demand that the question be answered.

*Nuance:* Resolve to be independent. Be willing to fight—fiercely, destructively—for independence. Yet accept the necessity of having to go on living after independence had been gained.

Adams believed that his task was both to incite and to control human passion. This was his nuanced understanding of revolution. His unflinching, uncompromising advocacy of independence—absolute and by all means necessary—marked him in the world of 1775–1776 as a radical, yet the revolution he so radically proposed was inherently conservative. That didn't mean "moderate" or "middle way." It meant conservative in the root sense of the word.

In his *Dissertation on the Canon and Feudal Law,* published in 1765 during the Stamp Act crisis, Adams explained that liberty was not an ideal, something to be created, something radically new in the world, but, rather, a set of rights "derived from our Maker," rights "indisputable, unalienable, indefeasible," as well as "inherent," "essential," and "divine," rights, moreover, guaranteed since the Middle Ages by nothing less than British law. As Adams saw it, there was no need of revolution to create or enact new rights, but every need for revolution to restore rights that were being withheld. Nor were the American colonies unique in having been deprived of existing rights. In a series of essays he signed "Novanglus" (New Englander), written in 1774–1775, Adams pointed to the example of Ireland, warning his fellow Americans that to accept tyranny in any form now could lead to the more brutal subjugation England had already visited upon the Irish, reducing the people to a potatoes-and-water subsistence.

Tear down, by all means, yes. But tear down only that which separates Americans from their rights. Then be sure to build new institutions that will guarantee access to those rights. Crown and Parliament, Adams would argue, were the true radicals for daring to deny ancient, even divine (and therefore timeless) rights. The American revolutionaries, in contrast, were the true conservatives, intent on restoring and then protecting—conserving—those rights.

It was not an easy concept, this tearing down in order to build, this radical conservatism. To bring the concept to realization, Adams honed and championed a two-chambered Congress, the establishment of a strong chief executive, and an independent judiciary, a government, in short, of three discrete branches whose powers checked and balanced one another. After the Revolution, Adams served George Washington as vice president, then, in succeeding him, continued to shape the presidency in Washington's image, seeking, as the first president had sought, to elevate the office above partisan politics. But he was no mere post-Washington caretaker. Controversially—and the controversy continues today—he acted to stem in America the tide of the French Revolution, in which his one-time boon colleague and now archrival Jefferson saw the apotheosis of liberty, but in which Adams saw only anarchy and terror: the tyranny of nature's mob, the pulling down without the faintest prospect of building up.

As president, Adams promoted the Alien and Sedition Acts, legislation intended to stave off destructive French-inspired radicalism but also potentially so repressive as to repeal, in effect, many of the gains won in the American Revolution. Yet Adams was never apologetic about this. "I humbled the French Directory," he declared late in life, "as much as all Europe has humbled Bonaparte. I purchased navy yards. . . . built frigates, manned a navy, and selected officers with great anxiety and care, who perfectly protected our commerce, and gained virgin victories against the French," with whom an undeclared naval war had broken out. At home, President Adams "engaged in the most earnest, sedulous, and, I must own, expensive exertions to preserve peace with the Indians. . . . Not a hatchet was lifted in my time." On the diplomatic front, the second president, by his own account, "finished the demarcation of limits, and settled all controversies with Spain. I made the composition [settlement] with England, for all the old Virginia debts, and all the other American debts." In sum:

*I had complete and perfect success, and left my country at peace with all the world, upon terms consistent with the honor and interest of the United States, and with all our relations with other nations, and all our obligations by the law of nations or by treaties. . . .*

*I left navy yards, fortifications, frigates, timber, naval stores, manufactories of cannon and arms, and a treasury full of five millions of dollars. This was all done step by step, against perpetual oppositions, clamors and reproaches, such as no other President ever had to encounter, and with a more feeble, divided, and incapable support than has ever fallen to the lot of any administration before or since.*

No historian would disagree with this self-assessment, the judgment of a man hard on rivals and friends alike, and hardest of all on himself, a man even his bitterest enemies conceded was above all brutally honest and honorable. He was not, nor ever could be, an icon, a monumental image. He was a real-world, flesh-and-blood political leader, a man who endeavored not merely to incite a revolution, but to manage it, to bring change and yet to control change.

Adams was a steward of justice and liberty. His leadership was less about change than about just and effective sustainability, and it is for this reason that his experience offers to those who lead and manage modern enterprises such rich, relevant, and immediately useful lessons. For the more a business changes and must respond to change—the more revolutionary a business must become—the more and more effectively its leaders must answer the question always uppermost in the mind of John Adams, *Then what?*

# CHAPTER I

# *"Mausoleums, Statues, Monuments Will Never Be Erected to Me"*

⟶ THE PRINCIPAL ARCHITECTS OF THE American Revolution came chiefly from two regions, Virginia and New England. Although united in the cause of independence, they might otherwise have been beings from different worlds. Virginia was a land of great plantations. Men like Washington, Jefferson, and Madison referred to it as their "country," and it spawned expansive, even imperial visions. New England, in craggy contrast, was a patchwork of small farms tended by yeoman farmers. Insular, it was conducive to looking inward, producing a state of mind more intellectual than imperial. If George Washington, intrepid soldier and bold wilderness surveyor, was the representative man of Virginia, John Adams was the exemplar of New England values: modest, prudent, economical, chaste—nearly ascetic—introspective, spiritual, and often relentlessly self-critical. Much of the greatness of the likes both of Washington and Adams lay in their having imbibed deeply of the qualities peculiar to the places of their birth and upbringing, yet also in their commensurate ability and willingness to transcend local allegiances to envision and create a single nation capable of encompassing worlds so different.

Born on October 30, 1735, John Adams was the eldest of three sons of a Braintree, Massachusetts, farmer and cobbler. That man, also named John Adams, was a fourth-generation American, his ancestor, Henry Adams, having immigrated from Barton St.

David in Somerset, England, to the Massachusetts Bay Colony about the year 1636. Susanna, wife of the senior John Adams, was also of a long-established New England family, the Boylstons, and nevertheless the junior John Adams, although a fifth-generation American, would grow into manhood looking every inch the stout, sturdy *English* yeoman, as if his physical being preserved his heritage undiluted.

His aspiration as a youth was to be neither more nor less than a farmer. His father held other ambitions for the boy, however, and wanted him to get an education in preparation for Harvard College and the ministry. When young Adams persisted in expressing his desire to farm, his father responded by heaping upon him a multitude of farm chores in the hope that he would be rapidly discouraged; but his son was both stubborn and strong.

"Well, John, are you satisfied with being a farmer?" his father asked him after a long day's labor.

"I like it very well, sir."

Doubtless frustrated yet entirely undaunted, the senior Adams replied, "Aya, but I don't like it so well: so you will go back to school today."

Before we jump to the conclusion that in this abortive contest between childish will and parental authority a revolutionary was born, we must recognize that the senior Adams proved no tyrant. Although he saw to it that his son continued his education, he listened when the boy told him somewhat later that it was not school he disliked, just the teacher. Mr. Adams promptly relocated his son to a private school, whose gifted pedagogue, one Joseph Marsh, immediately kindled a love of learning in his new student, and, at the age of fifteen, John Adams was fully prepared to enroll in Harvard College. He was much comforted by the thought that Marsh would accompany him to Cambridge, where he was to take the entrance examination, but when it came time to make the journey, the schoolmaster took ill and told his student that he must go to the Harvard examiners on his own.

John Adams was terrified by the prospect. Yet he recognized within himself a far worse terror: the fear of disappointing both his teacher and his father. That greater fear vanquished the lesser. He mounted his father's horse, and, all alone, rode off to Cambridge. After taking the examination, he was not only admitted, but granted a partial scholarship. His father, greatly gratified, sold ten acres of his farmland to finance the balance of his son's education the scholarship failed to cover.

Like New England itself, the Harvard of 1751 was a place of intimate proportions, consisting of seven professors and four brick buildings in addition to a tiny chapel. Adams's Class of 1755 included twenty-seven scholars in all—of whom none, doubtless, loved the place more than John Adams did. He "read forever," he later recalled, acquiring a love of books that would last his whole life. But one passion he did not acquire was a hunger for the ministry, and, rather than pursue ordination after his graduation, he decided to teach school for a few years, finding employment in Worcester, Massachusetts, and proving himself a most humane schoolmaster for the time. He seldom scolded his dozen or so charges and even more rarely wielded the rod upon them. He believed positive encouragement a stronger incentive to achievement than either harsh words or the sting of hickory, yet, as it would be in the future, his philosophy was tempered with carefully considered nuance. Praise, by all means, yet "be cautious and sparing of . . . praise, lest it become too familiar."

Whatever of value he imparted to his handful of scholars, his time as a teacher was mostly a period of pondering his choice of "real" career. No, it would not be the ministry. Instead, he apprenticed to James Putnam, a successful Worcester lawyer, and in 1758 was himself admitted to the bar. It was a choice in which his father did not rejoice, yet did acquiesce just the same.

Not that John Adams had abandoned religion. For him, the law *was* religion. It was about morality, justice, reward, and punishment. It was a vision of order in the universe. It was, most of all, a means of governing—in the most literal sense of the word, managing—life. In August 1763, Adams made his debut in print with an essay called "On Private Revenge," published in the *Boston Gazette*. All that truly set humanity apart from the beasts, Adams wrote, was the "capacity of uniting with others," including in the agreement to settle all dispute by law. Without this capacity—and without the allegiance to law this capacity enabled—each person "must be his own avenger." Offended, one had no choice but to "fall to fighting. . . . teeth . . . nails . . . feet, or fists, or, perhaps, the first club or stone that can be grasped, must decide the contest, by finishing the life of one." Such was human existence without the religion of law. From the beginning of his adult career, John Adams dedicated himself to liberty and justice, but he understood these to be far more than a matter of mere freedom. They required individuals to unite themselves into a society and, moreover, to unite under law. True justice, true liberty demanded restraint as much as freedom. The key was that this restraint must issue from no man (that would be tyranny) but from the law.

For Adams, there was life and there was law. As in any equation, both were equally important and had to be made to balance. Adams became as voracious an observer of human behavior and human character in the flesh as he was a reader of human history on the printed page. He filled diaries and notebooks with descriptions of day-to-day events and his impressions of men. At the same time, he was omnivorous in his study of law, basing his understanding of it both on recent and ongoing cases as well as on the past, on precedents reaching back to the Greeks and Romans.

It was, of course, the law that ushered John Adams into the cause of independence. As a young lawyer, he deeply admired one of Boston's most prominent and most eloquent attorneys, James Otis.

Adams was present, taking copious notes, in February 1761 when Otis argued before the Council Chamber of Massachusetts Province House, Boston, against the legality of the Writs of Assistance, the general warrants that allowed Crown officials to search at will for smuggled material within any suspected premises and without any warrant. The issue, Otis argued, was that Parliament could make no legislation relating to the American colonies because those colonies were not represented in Parliament. From this point forward, Adams's passion for the law became inextricably bound up with his growing belief that colonial independence was not merely desirable, but necessary—necessary under law, necessary to attain and preserve justice, and therefore necessary to civilized life itself. The alternative to independence was the alternative to law, justice, and true civilization. It was tyranny.

●　●　●

In 1764, John Adams married Abigail Smith, daughter of a Weymouth, Massachusetts, Congregational minister and a woman of great intelligence and intense curiosity. The pair, deeply in love, were also intellectual partners, whose lifelong correspondence is a tender and eloquent exchange of emotion and ideas. They had six children, of whom one died at birth and another, John Quincy (1767–1848), was destined to become the sixth president of the United States.

In contrast to most of history's revolutions, the American War of Independence was not a revolt of the downtrodden masses against an oppressive ruling class. Instead, it was organized and led by members of the most prosperous classes of American colonial society—wealthy planters and rich merchants. John Adams was neither of these, but his law practice grew rapidly and he earned a handsome living from it. Like the other founding fathers, he had a substantial financial stake in American colonial society, and, like them, he was willing to risk that stake for the sake of liberty. Nevertheless, during his years of service first to the cause of independence and then to the fledgling government of the newly independent United States, Adams remained acutely aware of the financial and personal sacrifices he was making and, furthermore, that he was compelling his wife and family to make.

The young attorney entered the political arena when he stepped to the forefront as one of the opponents of the Stamp Act of 1765. The most egregious of revenue and regulatory legislation Parliament enacted in an effort to defray some of the expenses of the late French and Indian War and the ongoing necessity of defending the North American colonies, the Stamp Act required colonists to purchase tax stamps for all documents and paper products, ranging from deeds and promissory notes to ordinary stationery and playing cards. The stamps were not cheap. Those applied to certain legal documents brought fees as high as £10, the equivalent of hundreds of dollars today. Not only were the taxes authorized by the Stamp Act burdensome, their administration and enforcement were put into the hands of Crown functionaries rather than colonial officials. Thus, a tax imposed by a Parliament in which the colonies were unrepresented was administered and enforced by men who answered not to the American people but to the Parliament and the king. To Adams and others, the Stamp Act was the very incarnation of tyranny.

Adams drafted instructions that the citizens of Braintree sent to their representatives in the Massachusetts legislature, outlining the rationale for opposition to the Stamp Act. The document immediately became the model on which other New England towns drew when they composed instructions to their own representatives. In this way, Adams became instrumental in uniting opposition against a major policy of the mother country, and in this way, too, his reputation began to spread beyond the confines of Braintree and even New England. Adams's instructions fully articulated the most momentous and salient reason for opposing the Stamp Act: that it denied to Americans two of the most basic rights guaranteed to all Englishmen—the right to be taxed only by consent (that is, the right to representation in Parliament), and the right to be tried by a jury of one's peers (a right denied because enforcement of the Stamp Act was a matter for the Admiralty Court, a royal rather than colonial institution).

During the summer of 1765, Adams anonymously published his second major political work, four articles that appeared in the *Boston Gazette* and which became known collectively in America as *A Dissertation on the Canon and Feudal Law* and, in England (where the *London Chronicle* picked them up in 1768), more provocatively, as *True Sentiments of America*. In this, Adams greatly expanded his consideration of the significance and necessity of opposing the Stamp Act. Not only was the legislation illegal, it violated the very spirit of America by going against the reasons that had motivated Adams's own Puritan ancestors to sail to the continent in the seventeenth century: freedom from tyranny. Adams thus elevated opposition to the Stamp Act from the status of protest against a particular tax at a particular time to a genuinely spiritual and moral cause, both patriotic and timeless. In his *Dissertation*, he made opposition to the Stamp Act an occasion for coming together as a new people.

Adams's public opposition to the Stamp Act culminated in December 1765, when he delivered a speech before the governor and colonial council asserting that the legislation was invalid, null, and void because Massachusetts, unrepresented in Parliament, had not assented to it. Thanks to Adams—and others—the colonies did unite in resistance to the Stamp Act, forcing Parliament to repeal it. That repeal temporarily quieted the stirrings of revolution, but it certainly did not extinguish them.

Had John Adams been a simpler and more straightforward revolutionary zealot, like his second cousin Samuel Adams, he would have welcomed the next crisis, which came less than five years after the Stamp Act repeal. In 1769, a dispute over the Royal Navy's practice of "impressing" young men into naval service—abducting them from Boston wharfs and involuntarily inducting them into His Majesty's service as sailors—combined with attempts by royal customs collectors to seize the *Liberty*, a provocatively named merchant ship owned by John Hancock, prompted the Crown to dispatch two regiments of British infantry to Boston.

They were emphatically unwelcome. Yet while Bostonians regarded the redcoats as agents of royal tyranny, the soldiers were also victims of that tyranny. Subjected to brutal discipline— "lobsterbacks," the colonists called them, because they bore vivid welts inflicted by the lash—the troops were paid a miserable wage and were chronically in want. On a cold, gray March 5, 1770, one desperate lobsterback presented himself at Grey's Ropewalk—a wharfside maker of ship's ropes—hoping to find part-time work. It was hard times for soldier and civilian alike, as Boston and the rest of the country struggled in the harsh economic recession that followed the French and Indian War. When a small crowd that had clustered around the ropewalk saw a British soldier, agent of oppression, trying to rob them of a precious job, a small riot erupted. It quickly subsided, but the mob remained out and about, growing in size, and finally gathering around one Hugh White, a British sentry posted to guard the Customs House.

They had been drawn to White by the complaint of Bostonian Edward Garrick, who had earlier proclaimed to the sentry that his company commander failed to pay his employer for a wig he had ordered. In an unfortunate spasm of military loyalty, White demanded that the accuser step forward. When Garrick did, the sentry rammed the butt of his musket into his face. Clapping hands to his bloody cheek, Garrick ran, pursued by another redcoat at the point of a bayonet. Hearing of this, the mob retaliated by hurling icy snowballs at White and other soldiers. By the time British officers arrived, redcoats and citizens were spoiling for a fight.

Captain Thomas Preston corralled seven soldiers to rescue Sentry White, but the mob surged forward, blocking him. Preston ordered his detachment to form a defensive line where they stood. The Bostonians responded with yet more ice balls, daring the soldiers to open fire. Preston summoned Justice of the Peace James Murray, who read out the Riot Act, a move that provoked another volley of ice. Then someone hurled a heavy wooden club, which knocked Private Hugh Montgomery off his feet. Rising, he silently cocked his musket and fired into the crowd.

No one was hit, but a merchant named Richard Palmes struck out at Montgomery with a billet of wood. The redcoat lunged at him with his bayonet, sending Palmes back into the crowd. A roar went up, and Private Matthew Killroy leveled his musket at Edward Langford and Samuel Gray.

"God damn you, don't fire!" Gray protested, whereupon Killroy reflexively sent a musket ball into his brain.

Nearly at the same moment, another shot rang out. It was just a single shot, but the soldier, panicky, had apparently loaded his weapon twice. For two musket rounds dug into the chest of Crispus Attucks, a forty-year-old fugitive slave from Framingham, killing him instantly. Gray had taken the first shot—and he would later die—but historians count Attucks as the first to fall in the struggle for liberty.

The death of Attucks was followed by more shots. Two more Bostonians died instantly and a third was fatally wounded. As the soldiers reloaded, the mob again pressed forward. This time, Preston intervened, striding along the line of his men, knocking each musket barrel skyward and barking out, "Don't fire!"

A Massachusetts court was quick to indict Captain Preston and six of his men on charges of murder. The redcoats must certainly have believed themselves doomed to mob justice, and Sam Adams was willing to give them just that in the hope that the "Boston

Massacre"—his name for the incident—would blossom then and there into a full-scale revolution.

But John Adams, in company with fellow attorney Josiah Quincy, stepped forward with an offer to undertake the defense of the accused. Where his second cousin saw the trigger of revolution, John Adams saw the danger of a people who aspired to become a nation of genuine law and justice deny both law and justice. "Council," Adams declared, "ought to be the very last thing an accused person should want [be denied] in a free country." At the risk of alienating his fellow New Englanders, Adams delivered a brilliant defense, arguing justifiable homicide by reason of self-defense. In the end, it speaks eloquently of the attorneys as well as the Boston juries that Preston and four of his men were acquitted and two others were found guilty not of murder, but of the lesser crime of manslaughter. The Boston Massacre trials not only rescued the accused redcoats, they served to calm—yet again—revolutionary fervor.

But not for long. In 1772, Thomas Hutchinson, the royal governor of Massachusetts, issued a proclamation to the effect that judges' salaries would no longer be paid by the Massachusetts legislature, but would be furnished instead by Parliament from customs revenues. At the behest of Boston revolutionaries, Adams wrote "Two Replies of the Massachusetts House of Representatives to Governor Hutchinson," arguing against the proclamation by asserting that the colonists were not now and had never rightfully been under the sovereignty of Parliament. The colony's charter, he pointed out, had been granted by the king, to whom the colonists owed sole allegiance. Yet the king had no authority to tax or to pay salaries from taxes. Nor could he legally compel or coerce colonial subjugation to Parliament. Independence, therefore, emerged as the only viable course for the colonies.

Having laid this groundwork of a legal argument for independence, Adams followed it in 1774–1775 with a series of essays published in the *Boston Gazette* under the pseudonym Novanglus (New Englander). His concern was to expand the basis of law on which American independence could be built. In the *Novanglus* essays, Adams traced the history, the nature, and the application of the British "constitution," which was not a single document, but an accretion of law, common law, and tradition. He then demonstrated, on historical principles, how American provincial legislatures were effectively sovereign over their internal affairs and that the colonies were linked to England not through Parliament but only through the person of the king. The *Novanglus* essays did not make the case for complete independence, but, rather, implied the propriety of commonwealth status for the colonies. Nevertheless, it was clear that if the king would not accept this, total independence was the only viable course available.

Adams left to others the rabble-rousing. His purpose was to ensure that the revolution, when it came, would be justified in legal terms that Americans, liberal- and fair-minded Englishmen, and enlightened citizens of all the world would understand and embrace. The exercise of arbitrary tyranny—the rule of the mob—was not a proper instrument for the removal of royal or Parliamentary tyranny. Adams wanted to elevate the revolution above personal revenge and above the realm of mere human passion. He wanted to make it an exercise of law.

Adams's writings made him a natural choice as a Massachusetts delegate to the first and second Continental Congresses in 1774 and 1775–1778. It was Adams who, in June 1775, nominated George Washington as commander-in-chief of the so-called Boston Army, which held the British garrison under siege and which was soon transformed into the Continental Army. Adams based his nomination in part on Washington's military record in the French and Indian War, but, even more important, he believed that putting a Virginian in charge of a force that—at the time—consisted exclusively of New Englanders would do much to promote colonial unity and begin the transformation of the colonies from a collection of regions to a nation.

Adams worked tirelessly in Congress, serving on many committees, including the one that ultimately created a Continental Navy. Throughout his political career, Adams would be a champion of sea power and frequently spoke of defending the nation by means of "wooden walls"—the stout frigates of an American navy. Adams also worked behind the scenes, vigorously politicking and patiently shaping members' views toward absolute and permanent separation from the mother country. It was Adams who persuaded Thomas Jefferson to draft the Declaration of Independence, demurring from the task himself with a claim that Jefferson was the better writer (a debatable point) and that he was of a more amiable nature and therefore better liked (probably true). It is also the case that, like Washington, Jefferson was a Virginian, and Adams was anxious to prevent the revolution, concentrated at its opening in New England, from having too regional a flavor.

On May 15, 1776, the Continental Congress urged the colonies—now called states—to draft their own constitutions. For most of the states, this proved easier said than done. Today, we take for granted the importance of a constitution as the written framework of any government. In the eighteenth century, however, the idea of a constitution was in itself radical. Few of the world's governments were documented in a single text. The English "constitution" was a body of law and tradition, not a piece of paper. The states therefore looked to Congress for guidance, and it soon fell to Adams to issue advice. He digested his ideas into *Thoughts on Government*, a pamphlet published in 1776, which served many state legislatures as a road map to guide them through the composition of their constitutions. Whereas the author of the Declaration of Independence expressed himself—quite appropriately for the occasion—in lofty, idealistic, and timeless terms, Adams grappled more robustly with what a later generation would call *realpolitik*. He did not see an independent United States as a utopia of democratic government, but as a "mixed government," much as Aristotle had articulated. "All men are created equal," Jefferson had written. Adams understood that this applied to rights, not social station. He believed that, even though the United States would lack a titled aristocracy, it would hardly exist as a classless society. His thoughts on government were aimed at accommodating, equitably but practically, the reality of social classes. Adams sought to do this largely by ensuring that the American Republic would be governed by laws, not men. Laws were incorruptible, whereas people were not. To promote a government of laws, Adams advocated a bicameral legislature, which would balance purely democratic representation against republican representation—maintaining a popularly elected House of Representatives as well as a legislatively appointed Senate. In addition, this bicameral legislative branch of government would be balanced by equally independent executive and judicial branches, each of which would check and balance the other. Adams was concerned with managing democracy through republican government, which imposed checks, balances, and controls on liberty—yet which did so organically rather than arbitrarily, so that, by virtue of regulating liberty, liberty was defended, promoted, and preserved.

●  ●  ●

In the early phase of the American Revolution, Adams was instrumental in creating the pattern of domestic government. As the war progressed, in 1777—and again in 1779—Congress called on him to represent emerging American interests in Europe. On his second trip, he had the full authority of minister plenipotentiary and was tasked with negotiating peace with Britain as well as obtaining British recognition of independence. The government of America's chief ally, France, objected to the degree of power vested in Adams, and he was therefore compelled to share negotiating authority with

Benjamin Franklin, Thomas Jefferson, John Jay, and Henry Laurens. In actual practice, it was Adams, Jay, and Franklin who served as the key negotiators and, at that, Adams and Jay overrode the Francophile Franklin so that they could deal directly with the British treaty commissioners rather than submit to the intermediary will of France. This bold step ensured that the interests of the United States—not those of France—would be paramount in the Treaty of Paris, signed on November 30, 1782, which formally ended the American Revolution early the following year.

Even while treaty negotiations were ongoing, Adams traveled to the Netherlands, at the time the world's only other fully functional republic, in an effort to secure recognition, a commercial treaty, and a substantial loan. In all of this, Adams succeeded, establishing at the Hague the first embassy of the United States. Thus it was John Adams who effectively founded the United States diplomatic corps and foreign service. In 1785, Adams next took up the challenging post of first U.S. ambassador to the Court of St. James's—ambassador to Great Britain—and managed to establish at least tenuously civil relations between the United States and its former mother country.

Before he left on his foreign assignments, Adams had composed a new republican constitution for the State of Massachusetts. Although the document was modified by committee, it remained largely the work of Adams, who embodied in it all that he had stated more theoretically in his *Thoughts on Government.* The constitution introduced a bicameral legislature, an executive branch—a governor with partial veto powers (overriding the veto required a two-thirds vote of the legislature)—and an independent judicial branch. The Massachusetts constitution would exert a profound influence on those who drafted the new United States Constitution. While abroad, in 1787, Adams published *A Defence of the Constitutions of Government of the United States,* in which he elaborated on the utility of a bicameral legislature, explaining that the "upper house" would naturally be composed chiefly of the wealthy and wellborn and would be balanced and checked by the "lower house," which would be more representative of the masses. Adams sought specifically to counter arguments against instituting bicameral legislatures in republics, pointing out that the mere fact of creating a republic—dispensing with hereditary rulers—did not level the social classes. A two-chambered legislature took social reality into account and dealt with it as equitably as possible. "Power," Adams wrote, "must be opposed to power, and interest to interest."

Under the new national Constitution, George Washington was unanimously elected the first president of the United States. In effect by acclamation and prearrangement, John Adams received the second-highest number of votes in the electoral college and thus became vice president in 1789 and again in 1792. He served Washington faithfully, but was frustrated by the office, writing to Abigail that his "country has in its wisdom contrived for me the most insignificant office that ever the invention of man contrived or his imagination conceived." While it is true that President Washington rarely if ever consulted him on matters of policy, Adams did preside with vigor over the Senate, casting thirty-one tie-breaking votes—a record yet to be shattered. The votes Adams cast enhanced the power of the executive branch, ensuring that the president would have sole authority over the removal of his own appointees. One of his tie-breaking votes was also instrumental in permanently locating the nation's capital in the District of Columbia. Even more significantly, he acted like a senator himself, pressuring others to vote his way and endlessly lecturing the Senate on matters of procedure. Some felt that he was unduly imposing the prerogatives of the executive branch on the legislative, and by the end of his first term as vice president, Adams was compelled to retreat somewhat. His second term presiding over the Senate was marked by greater restraint.

As vice president, Adams also became embroiled in a controversy over what the official title of the president should be. Desiring to endow the chief executive with a certain loftiness, Adams pushed for such titles as "His High Mightiness" and "His Majesty the President," disdaining the simple "Mr. President" and "President of the United States." His position became a target for popular satire, and because Vice President Adams had put on significant weight with late middle age, some in the press bestowed on him the unflattering title of "His Rotundity."

Although Washington had counseled his fellow countrymen against creating divisive political parties, they were quickly formed nevertheless. Adams became a charter member of the Federalist Party, which supported a strong central government with a powerful chief executive, and which was opposed by the party of Thomas Jefferson, the Democratic-Republicans, who advocated more democracy and less republicanism, with power vested less in a central government than in the states themselves and in the people of those states. Federalist though he was, Adams remained wary of his party's most dynamic leader, Alexander Hamilton, who, he believed, was hyper-ambitious and, therefore, dangerous—a threat to the concept of government of law instead of government of men. It was Adams and not Hamilton who became the Federalists' first standard bearer, narrowly winning election as second president of the United States in 1796 with seventy-one electoral votes to Thomas Jefferson's sixty-eight. Under the law of the time, runner-up Jefferson assumed the office of vice president. Former revolutionary colleagues and close friends, Adams and Jefferson now stood at opposite ends of the political spectrum, a situation that made for an uneasy working relationship.

As president, Adams cleaved to Washington's policy of refusing to be sucked into the war between the French and the British. This put him at odds with much prevailing popular sentiment, which favored France on account of the late Franco-American revolutionary alliance against Britain. The so-called Jay Treaty, negotiated with Britain in 1794 during the Washington administration, had alienated the French, who perceived the treaty as the beginning of an Anglo-American alliance against them. This touched off undeclared naval warfare in which French ships seized American merchantmen trading with the British. Anxious to avoid outright war, Adams sent a commission to negotiate with France. Yet, ever the realist, he hedged his bet on the successful outcome of the commission, appealing to Congress to increase funding for the army and, especially, the navy. It was a good thing that he did so, because the commission was not even received by the Directory—the governing body of revolutionary France—a rebuff that led to the notorious XYZ Affair, in which personal bribes were imperiously demanded as a precondition of diplomatic negotiation. Amid sharply deteriorating Franco-American relations, the undeclared naval warfare escalated into what historians call the Quasi-War, also undeclared, but often quite intense. Thanks in large part to Adams's advocacy and support, the fledgling U.S. Navy triumphed repeatedly against French men o' war.

Whereas Jefferson and his Democratic-Republicans favored radically revolutionary France, Adams and his Federalists feared that nation and worried that the United States would be swept by the contagion of mob rule. The Federalists in Congress passed the Alien and Sedition Acts—all signed by the president in 1798—which included the Naturalization Act, the Alien Act, the Alien Enemies Act, and the Sedition Act. The Naturalization Act more than doubled the period required to naturalize foreign-born individuals seeking American citizenship, raising the interval from five to fourteen years. It was, in fact, a naked attempt to cripple the Democratic-Republican Party, because most newly naturalized immigrants voted for the members of that party. The Alien Act empowered the president to deport any alien he deemed dangerous to the country, and the Alien Enemies Act permitted the arrest, imprisonment, and deportation in wartime of any alien subject to an enemy power. Most controversial of all, the Sedition Act defined as a treasonable high misdemeanor the publication of "any false, scandalous and malicious writing" critical of the government or government officials. Under this frank abridgment of freedom of speech, some twenty-five individuals, almost all of them editors of Republican newspapers, were prosecuted and their papers forced to shut down. Although it is true that none of the Alien and Sedition Acts originated with Adams and that he did not champion them, he did sign them, and he did make use of them, leading Democratic-Republicans to condemn him as what they called a "monarchist."

The fact was that, far from being monarchist or dictatorial, Adams increasingly found himself at odds with the right wing of his own Federalist Party, the so-called High Federalists, who sought to amass ever more centralized power in the government. Adams was particularly alarmed by Alexander Hamilton, leader of the High Federalists, who, becoming second in command of the army, essentially seized control of the War Department. Led by Hamilton, High Federalist legislators continually challenged and undermined Adams's authority. Although Adams had recalled George Washington to command the army, the High Federalist faction demanded that Hamilton be given actual control of the military, and they blocked Adams's even-handed attempts to appoint some Democratic-Republicans—most notably Aaron Burr—to senior command positions in the army. Although he opposed the liberalism of the Democratic-Republicans, Adams was more fearful of fatally dividing the government and of giving too much power, especially control of the military, to a single party and, indeed, to a faction within that party. He believed in the basic Federalist agenda, to be sure, but he did not want the party used as a short-term tool to gain power. Rather, he wanted Federalist ideals to permeate the structure of the nation, and if that meant compromising with the other party in the short term, so be it. Adams was far more interested in building a nation than in promoting a political party.

Whereas the High Federalists sought to expand the Quasi-War with France as an excuse to further build up the navy and the army, which they controlled, Adams, in February 1799, sent William Vans Murray to negotiate peace with France. Napoleon, who had risen to a controlling position during the wars of the French Revolution, had no desire to see the United States join with England against him, and he showed himself willing to negotiate. The result was a pair of new treaties, which superseded the Treaty of Alliance concluded during the American Revolution in 1778. Thus Adams not only ended the Quasi-War and averted a larger war, he also freed the United States from its entanglement with France while simultaneously reestablishing friendly relations with that country.

It was a great achievement, but it came at a cost. Much of the nation—and certainly many in Adams's own party—wanted war. Adams, however, set about dismantling the "emergency" army the High Federalists had assembled. He was determined to reestablish government of law rather than men—especially men backed by force of arms.

President John Adams must be credited with sacrificing his own power and the support of a major faction of his own party for the good of the new nation. Yet while this manager of revolution exercised profound and selfless leadership in this action, he made what many consider a fundamental management error in having retained for his Cabinet most of Washington's men. His rationale for this was reasonable. Washington had been elected by acclamation and was a hero larger than life. Adams had been reluctant to stir worries over an orderly succession and saw the retention of the Washington Cabinet as a means of easing the transition and creating a national sense of continuity. It took high character to resist simply impressing his own stamp on the Cabinet. Nevertheless, men like Hamilton were loyal to their conception of Washington's Federalism and were not willing to submit to the will of the new president.

The sudden death of George Washington in 1799 furnished stark evidence of the wisdom of Adams's efforts to shift power from men to laws. The Federalist Party never recovered from the loss of this man, from whom the party had derived most of its unity. Adams ran for reelection in 1800, but lost to Thomas Jefferson, less because of the rising popularity of Jefferson's Democratic-Republican Party than because of Hamilton's leadership of the High Federalists against him. To be sure, Adams's support of the Alien and Sedition Acts was unpopular, but had the Federalists remained unified, he would have defeated Jefferson. Adams's electoral college defeat was narrow at sixty-five to seventy-three votes.

Intent on leaving some lasting influence of Federalist thought and policy on what would soon be Jefferson's government, Adams appointed a number of judges during the closing days of his term. The Democratic-Republicans derided these men as "Midnight Judges," although Adams had actually appointed most of them weeks before the expiration of his term. Once installed in office, Jefferson managed to dispose of most of the appointees by simply abolishing their offices. But the new president could not depose John Marshall, whom Adams had nominated as chief justice of the Supreme Court in January 1801. It was through Marshall that Adams bequeathed not only to the Jefferson administration but to the history of the nation the most significant and enduring elements of Federalism.

. . .

John Adams retired from public life after his defeat for reelection and took up the career that he had told his father most appealed to him: working his Quincy, Massachusetts, farm. His political differences with Jefferson, with whom he had developed a close personal relationship during the Revolution, drove the two men apart and kept them that way until 1812, when Adams initiated a fourteen-year correspondence with his old friend that stands as a monument to American literature, autobiography, and political discourse. Among the many themes Adams and Jefferson explored in their letters were those revolving around what Jefferson called "natural aristocracy." Jefferson believed in the extensive perfectibility of humankind and trusted that, in a free government, the most able would inevitably rise to power, creating a government by natural aristocracy. Adams disagreed. Placing faith in the inevitable emergence of a natural aristocracy, he argued, was no way to govern a nation. The problem, he wrote, was that "Birth and wealth are conferred on some men as imperiously by nature, as genius, strength, or beauty," and birth and wealth inevitably create an artificial but hereditary de facto aristocracy, which may interfere with and suppress the so-called natural aristocracy. Fate or mere accident would always and repeatedly act to endow some men with great power and influence, regardless of their natural talents, wisdom, or virtue. Yes, he agreed with Jefferson, some people are naturally fit to lead, but reality by no means ensured that these would inevitably rise to power. Effective government had no choice but to take reality into account by providing for the rise of people of varying abilities and motives.

Adams lived to see the death of his son Charles, from alcoholism, in 1800, the death of his daughter Abigail—called Nabby—from breast cancer in 1816, and the death of his much-adored wife, Abigail, in 1818. But he also lived to see his son John Quincy Adams become the sixth president of the United States in 1825, some eighteen months before his own death on July 4, 1826. John Adams's final words, broken and incomplete, spoken very late in the afternoon, betokened reconciliation and a hope for enduring national unity: "Jefferson—still—surv—"

He did not know that his friend—and adversary—had himself died a few hours earlier at Monticello.

# CHAPTER 2

# Motivation

### Lesson 1

## MANAGE BY MOTIVATION

*I find, by repeated experiment and observation in my school, that human nature is more easily wrought upon and governed by promises, and encouragement, and praise, than by punishment, and threatening, and blame. But we must be cautious and sparing of our praise, lest it become too familiar and cheap, and so, contemptible.*

—Diary, February 21, 1756

After graduating from Harvard and having abandoned his father's ambition for him—to enter the ministry—John Adams became a schoolmaster. In part, he had deliberately chosen this profession not as a calling but as an interim occupation, something to do while he decided on a life's work; yet he also dedicated himself to being as good a teacher as he could be, and, as in everything he did, he observed and he learned.

During the three years in which he taught school, Adams studied and regarded his young charges as a body of humanity to be governed and guided. In his diary, he wrote almost nothing about pedagogical theory, other than recording his belief that it was best to spare the rod and be more liberal with praise. He did not presume to announce that he had devised effective methods of motivating *students* or *children,* but he did note his discovery of a principle of "human nature." Even among mere schoolchildren, Adams could not avoid drawing momentous conclusions. Like a scientist, he practiced inductive reasoning, formulating far-reaching philosophical principles from the homeliest of firsthand observations.

He discovered that positive and desirable commodities— promises, encouragement, and praise—were better motivators than negative consequences: punishment, threats, and blame. He concluded specifically that this was true not merely of children, but of humanity generally. Certainly, it is a lesson that all effective managers learn sooner or later—the most effective sooner rather than later. Typically of Adams, however, he did not stop with this discovery. For Adams, truths rarely existed in isolation. For him, the principles that govern life generally came in opposing pairs. For every positive, there was a negative and vice versa. Thus Adams saw the weakness of praise as well as its strength. Praise was a definite good, but, administered too liberally, it became cheap, contemptible, and therefore no longer effective as a motivator.

**The Last Word:** Praise and other rewards are powerful forces for management, but, Adams understood, like any other force, they must themselves be well managed.

## Lesson 2
## AVOW YOUR OPINIONS AND DEFEND THEM WITH BOLDNESS

*Honesty, sincerity, and openness I esteem essential marks of a good mind. I am, therefore, of opinion that men ought, (after they have examined with unbiased judgments every system of religion, and chosen one system, on their own authority, for themselves,) to avow their opinions and defend them with boldness.*

—Diary, March 7, 1756

For Adams, received wisdom was not wisdom at all. Take religion. Whereas most people followed the faith of their parents—the faith they had been taught and taught in the absence of any other— Adams believed that choice of religion should be the work of an honest, sincere, and open mind thoroughly investigating "every system of religion" before settling on one to adopt for oneself. Yet once the decision has been made, it should be explained and defended boldly, without reservation.

True belief is fully informed belief, arrived at without coercion, bias, or prejudgment and with a thorough awareness of all the options. Although each individual should form his own opinions and render his own judgments, he should also put them out into the world by expressing and defending them. If everyone acquired religion or other profound knowledge in this manner, the state of human knowing would be rapidly advanced as arguments and perceptions were expressed, shared, criticized, and modified, all in the spirit of free inquiry.

It is one thing to lead toward consensus and united effort, but quite another to demand orthodox conformity of thought. As the leader of an enterprise, the last thing you want is for everyone to think the same way. This, in effect, reduces the potential creativity of any ten people to that of just one. The object is to leverage your human assets, not to minimize them.

*Revolutionary Wisdom*

"Oh! That I could wear out of my mind every mean and base affectation; conquer my natural pride and self conceit; expect no more deference from my fellows than I deserve; acquire that meekness and humility which are the sure mark and characters of a great and generous soul; subdue every unworthy passion, and treat all men as I wish to be treated by all. How happy should I then be in favor and good will of all honest men and the sure prospect of a happy immortality!"

—*Diary, February 16, 1756*

**The Last Word:** Encourage individual thought and evaluation, but demand that these be shared with everyone in the organization, subjected to examination, criticism, and refinement—all with the object of making the best choices in matters of creativity, management, ethics, and all other aspects of conducting a productive enterprise.

## Lesson 3
## PRESIDE, BESTOW, BLAME, PUNISH, AND INSPIRE

*In short, my little school, like the great world, is made up of kings, politicians, divines, L.D.'s [doctors of law], fops, buffoons, fiddlers, sycophants, fools, coxcombs, chimney sweepers, and every other character drawn in history, or seen in the world. Is it not, then, the highest pleasure . . . to preside in this little world, to bestow the proper applause upon the virtuous and generous actions, to blame and punish every vicious and contracted trick, to wear out of the tender mind every thing that is mean and little, and fire the new-born soul with a noble ardor and emulation?*

—Diary, March 15, 1756

Fascinated by the notion of his classroom as a microcosm of society, with himself in charge of it all, John Adams was beguiled most by the opportunity he was given to observe human behavior precisely and close-up and to shape that behavior by rewarding what was desirable in his little world and punishing what was not. Yet he did not stop at a simple scheme of reward and punishment. Adams also recognized his responsibility to inspire his charges, fire their "new-born" souls with "noble ardor" and present to them the finest historical, intellectual, and moral models for emulation.

**The Last Word:** Effective management is unrelenting leadership, a strenuous task of close observation and evaluation, and a rigorous, objective application of reward, criticism, and inspiration. The objective is not to attempt to change or try to "fix" people, but to recognize what each has to offer, and to provide the feedback, guidance, rewards, and corrections that will tend to optimize the unique gifts of each. In this way, a manager can shape levels of individual performance that are most likely, in the aggregate, to advance the enterprise as a whole.

**Lesson 4**

## THE WEAKNESS OF FORCE

*The elephant and the lion, when their strength is directed and applied by man, can exert a prodigious force. But their strength, great and surprising as it is, can produce no great effects when applied by no higher ingenuity than their own.*

—Diary, May 17, 1756

For Adams, revolution had become a necessary force of change. But for Adams, the danger of revolution was the tendency of those who fomented and conducted it to wield it as pure force. Elephants and lions were capable of "prodigious force," but they lacked the ability to direct it and, therefore, were capable of producing "no great effects." Without the application of intelligence—direction, restraint, and control—force is ineffectual, weak, and, in the context of revolutionary change, merely destructive.

**The Last Word:** Leading any high-stakes enterprise requires force that is defined, guided, and restrained. As a manager of revolution, Adams left the accumulation of force to others and devoted himself to perfecting the intelligent means of converting force into an agent capable of producing "great effects."

## Lesson 5
## "Enthusiasm"

*I believe it will be found universally true, that no great enterprise for the honor or happiness of mankind was ever achieved without a large mixture of that noble infirmity.*

—*A Dissertation on the Canon and Feudal Law,* 1765

In the eighteenth century, the word *enthusiasm* meant more than mere excitement or interest in a subject. It connoted genuine possession by the spirit of God or, possibly, mere religious fanaticism. That is, the concept that *enthusiasm* embodied was suspect, descriptive of a state oscillating between genuine inspiration and dangerous zealotry. Adams, in most respects a profoundly rational individual, did not use the word lightly. His belief that "no great enterprise" was ever achieved without a generous helping of that "noble infirmity" enthusiasm anticipated by nearly a century Ralph Waldo Emerson's remarkably similar declaration—"Nothing great was ever achieved without enthusiasm"—which is, however, far less surprising coming from that romantic poet-philosopher's pen.

The fact is that Adams distrusted "passions" and "enthusiasms," but he certainly never discounted, let alone rejected, them. By the Stamp Act crisis of 1765, John Adams understood that a revolution, when it came, would be the product of reasoned argument and outright enthusiasm, both essential to bringing about epochal change.

*Revolutionary Wisdom*

"What is the proper business of mankind in this life? We come into the world naked, and destitute of all the conveniences and necessaries of life; and if we were not provided for and nourished by our parents, or others, should inevitably perish as soon as born; we increase in strength of body and mind, by slow and insensible degrees; one third of our time is consumed in sleep, and three sevenths of the remainder is spent in procuring a mere animal sustenance; and if we live to the age of threescore and ten, and then sit down to make an estimate in our minds of the happiness we have enjoyed, and the misery we have suffered, we shall find, I am apt to think, that the overbalance of happiness is quite inconsiderable. We shall find that we have been, through the greatest part of our lives, pursuing shadows, and empty but glittering phantoms, rather than substances. We shall find that we have applied our whole vigor, all our faculties, in the pursuit of honor, or wealth, or learning, or some other such delusive trifle, instead of the real and everlasting excellencies of piety and virtue."

—*Diary, May 29, 1756*

**The Last Word:** Persuasive argument that operates in the realm of reason is a powerful and indispensable tool of leadership, but it is folly to neglect the emotions.

**Lesson 6**

Fight Tyranny with Knowledge

*[W]henever a general knowledge and sensibility have prevailed among the people, arbitrary government and every kind of oppression have lessened and disappeared in proportion.*
— *A Dissertation on the Canon and Feudal Law,* 1765

John Adams, who began his working life as a schoolteacher, had an unshakeable belief in the power of education. Tyranny, he wrote, succeeded only upon an ignorant people. The "Dark Ages"—called such because of the popular ignorance that characterized the era—were ruled by tyrants, but as "the people in the middle ages became more intelligent in general," the conquest of tyranny commenced. Liberation, however, did not come about because of the invention of new ideas, but because people became aware of their rights, which were nothing new, but, rather, "derived from the great Legislator of the universe" and which could not properly be "repealed or restrained by human laws."

For Adams, the great end of education was to connect people with their natural rights and all that these rights entailed. When this is done, a government, a nation, a society, regardless of how dynamic, earns the stability of a foundation of unchanging principle. Leadership by declaration, fiat, and decree is tyranny, and the organization it produces is arbitrary, requiring force and the fear of force to hold it together and perpetuate it. Like any other system that is not self-sustaining, the arbitrary enterprise is doomed to a short and minimally productive life, whereas a commonwealth, corporate or national, populated by the educated and the thoughtful continually renews itself in accordance with shared and changeless principles.

*Revolutionary Wisdom*

"The nature and essence of the material world is not less concealed from our knowledge than the nature and essence of God. We see ourselves surrounded on all sides with a vast expanse of heavens, and we feel ourselves astonished at the grandeur, the blazing pomp of those stars with which it is adorned. The birds fly over our heads and our fellow animals labor and sport around us; the trees wave and murmur in the winds; the clouds float and shine on high; the surging billows rise in the sea, and ships break through the tempest; here rises a spacious city, and yonder is spread out an extensive plain. These objects are so common and familiar that we think ourselves fully acquainted with them; but these are only effects and properties; the substance from whence they flow is hid from us in impenetrable obscurity."

—*Diary, July 31, 1756*

**The Last Word:** There is no advantage in seeking unthinking obedience.

**Lesson 7**
MAKE IT REAL

*We have called this a burthensome tax . . .*
—"Instructions of the Town of Braintree to Their Representative," 1765

During the Stamp Act crisis, John Adams prepared instructions—what today might be called "talking points"—to guide the town's colonial legislature representative in articulating opposition to the act. Published in the *Boston Gazette* on October 14, 1765, the "Instructions" were circulated, read, and adopted throughout the colonies.

Adams was a brilliant theorist, who eloquently framed the reasons first for protest, then for revolution in the enduring terms of principle, of right, of justice, and of liberty in conformity with "natural" right. Yet he never permitted himself or his audience to lose their footing on the ground of hard reality. The Stamp Act was wrong because, as taxation without representation, it was inherently tyrannical. Yet Adams knew that some people preferred tyranny to protest, let alone revolution, and he accordingly detailed how the act imposed a "burthensome tax" that created "embarrassments [obstacles] to business in this infant, sparsely-settled country so great, that it would be totally impossible for the people to subsist under it." The tax was not simply wrong in principle, Adams argued, it was economically lethal and "would drain the country of its cash, strip multitudes of their property, and reduce them to absolute beggary."

*Revolutionary Wisdom*

"Our minds are capable of receiving an infinite variety of ideas from those numerous material objects with which we are surrounded. . . . By curiously inquiring into the situation, fruits, produce, manufactures, &c., of our own, and by traveling into or reading about other countries, we can gain distinct ideas of almost every thing upon this earth, at present; and by looking at the history we can settle in our minds a clear and comprehensive view of this earth at its creation; of its various changes and revolutions; of its various catastrophes; of its progressive cultivation, sudden depopulation, and gradual repeopling; of the growth of several kingdoms and empires; of their wealth and commerce, wars and politics; of the characters of their principal leading men; of their grandeur and power; of their virtues and vices; and of their insensible decline at first, and of their swift destruction at last. . . . And after our minds are furnished with this ample store of ideas, far from feeling burdened or overloaded, our thoughts are more free, and active, and clearer than before, and we are capable of diffusing our acquaintance with things much further; we are not satiated with knowledge; our curiosity is only improved and increased; our thoughts rove beyond the visible diurnal sphere; they range through the heavens and lose themselves amidst a labyrinth of worlds; and, not contented with what is, they run forward into futurity, and search for new employment there."

—*Diary, August 7, 1756*

**The Last Word:** To lead any enterprise for the long run, you must appeal to principle. Nevertheless, the most immediately compelling means of persuasion almost always descends from principle to particulars. It is a mistake to rely exclusively on arguments from principle. Approach each member of the organization with a picture of cause and effect. Person by person, make your leadership count. Make your leadership immediate. Make it real.

## Lesson 8

## THE LANGUAGE OF BUSINESS

*The public money of this country is the toil and labor of the people.*
—"Instructions of the Town of Braintree to Their Representative," 1765

For John Adams, taxes were not simply financial, but represented the whole being and effort of the community: the very "toil and labor of the people." To administer them from sources unconnected with—because unrepresented by—the people was therefore profoundly immoral.

By characterizing the "public money of this country" as the "toil and labor of the people," Adams displayed fluency in the real language of government. A tax is not simply money, but toil, labor—life's energy. It is the property of the people contributed for the creation of the common good.

**The Last Word:** As Adams eloquently spoke the language of government, so successful leaders in business must be fluent in the language of business. Talk in terms of dollars made, dollars saved, dollars invested, dollars spent, dollars lost, always connecting these to time, toil, and labor. Whether in government or business, the great thing about money as a medium of communication is its power to represent the investment, foolish or wise, of life itself.

**Lesson 9**
## Do Something to Be Remembered

*The people should never rise without doing something to be remembered,*
*something notable and striking.*

—Diary, December 17, 1773

In 1770, colonial agitation, partly spearheaded by John Adams, prompted Parliament to repeal the so-called Townshend Acts, thereby eliminating all of the odious taxes on import commodities with the single exception of the tax on tea, retained at the insistence of King George III, who asserted his belief that "there must always be one tax" so as to preserve Parliament's right to tax the colonies. In practice, colonists readily evaded the tea tax by buying smuggled tea from Dutch sources. In the end, the tea tax was harder on Britain's struggling East India Company than on the colonists. Fortunately for the company, its directors were on intimate terms with Lord Frederick North, who functioned as George's prime minister. As of early 1773, the company had some seventeen million pounds of Indian tea languishing in its London warehouses, all of which would rot if the company could not begin shipping some to America. The problem presented to Lord North was this: How could Americans be compelled to buy East India Company tea instead of the smuggled Dutch product?

North proposed a solution based on the fact that the East India Company actually paid two taxes on its tea, one when it landed the cargo in Britain, whether for sale or transshipment elsewhere, and another when it landed in America. North drafted and engineered passage of the Tea Act (May 10, 1773), which forgave the first tax and reduced to three pennies a pound the tax due on landing tea in America. This brought the price of East India tea below that of the smuggled Dutch tea. North was confident that, for the colonists, economics would trump ideology, they would start buying English tea, and all talk of rebellion would fade. The added bonus? The financial salvation of the East India Company.

But North had badly misjudged the colonists and their situation. The Tea Act drove American merchants, who had been up to this point politically moderate, into the radical camp. The legislation directed the East India Company to sell its product only to government-designated consignees in the ports of New York, Charleston, Philadelphia, and Boston, thereby cutting out the American merchants. Backed by the merchants, the Committees of Correspondence—bands of revolutionaries—embarked on a campaign of intimidation against the tea consignees, forcing them out of Philadelphia, New York, and Charleston. In addition, American captains and harbor pilots refused to handle East India Company cargo, and tea ships were turned back to London from Philadelphia and New York before they could either land or unload. Although a ship was landed at Charleston, its tea cargo was impounded and deposited in a warehouse, where it would remain until 1776, when the Continental Congress auctioned it off to augment its meager war chest.

In Boston, three ships did land, but agents of the local Committee of Correspondence barred their unloading and demanded that they return to England. Massachusetts royal governor Thomas Hutchinson responded by refusing the permits that would allow the ships to leave the harbor. This standoff precipitated a meeting, on December 16, 1773, of the Committee of Correspondence in Boston's Old South Church. When Hutchinson stood firm, John Adams's fiery second cousin, Sam Adams, ascended the Old South pulpit to declare: "This meeting can do nothing more to save the country." At these words, a keening imitation of the Mohawk war cry was raised from outside the church, and 150 colonists, faces painted in the manner of Mohawk warriors, marched to Griffin's Wharf, climbed into waiting boats, rowed out to the three tea ships moored in Boston harbor, boarded each simultaneously, and threw overboard 342 tea chests valued at £10,000 (almost $1.7 million today).

On December 17, John Adams recorded in his diary the sense he had that the "Boston Tea Party" had instantly galvanized support for independence. "There is a dignity, a majesty, a sublimity, in this last [latest] effort of the patriots," Adams wrote. "This destruction of the tea is so bold, so daring, so firm, intrepid and inflexible, and it must have so important consequences, and so lasting, that I cannot but consider it as an epocha in history."

Yet—and for Adams there almost always and inevitably was a "yet"—the Boston Tea Party was "but an attack upon property." It had to be raised to a fully symbolic level, as a message that would be delivered clear across the Atlantic to the king and Parliament. Otherwise, it would serve only to bring a "similar exertion of popular power," which would "produce the destruction of lives." Adams understood that "many persons"—his own second cousin among them—"wish that as many dead carcasses were floating in the harbor, as there are chests of tea." For them, *that* would be the start of a revolution. But Adams believed that a "much less number of lives . . . would remove the causes of all our calamities," provided that the import of this protest registered with both friends and enemies in Britain.

Although John Adams typically approached the task of persuasion by marshalling facts and appealing to popular reason, he had a profound appreciation of symbolism and was convinced that certain actions—such as the Boston Tea Party—could bring about mass movement and epochal change. Today's managers are generally wary of symbolism. They prefer to confine themselves to the language of business, which is money—money to be made, to be saved, to be spent—and tend to dismiss the power of any other form of communication. In Adams's day and situation, the equivalent of these money-minded managers were the patriots who wanted to produce a high body count. *That*, they believed, would speak louder than any mere symbolism. Adams hoped they were wrong.

THE LAST WORD: John Adams hoped that memorable acts of protest could serve as the symbolic equivalent of and alternative to war. As it turned out, symbolism was not sufficient to win independence. War was needed. Yet Adams had been right to hope, and no leader can afford to overlook or minimize the potential of meaningful symbols in motivating action and bringing about the most profound changes.

**Lesson 10**
## The Logic of Liberty

*An English king had no right to be absolute over Englishmen out of the realm, any more than in it.*

—*Novanglus,* 1774–1775

Since 1215, when King John signed the Magna Carta, absolute monarchy ceased to exist in England, and the nation evolved into a constitutional monarchy. This meant that no English king ruled absolutely over the people of England. Logically, Adams argued, this constitutional limit applied to Englishmen "out of the realm" as well as within it. Leaving the confines of England did not magically deliver any person into the absolute power of the king. But neither did it deliver any Englishman from the obligation of allegiance to the king—provided the king remained within the confines of the covenant that was the English constitution. The instant he sought to abrogate the constitution by depriving the colonists of their liberties as English men and women, "they were released from their allegiance."

**The Last Word:** Created by the passage of time, familiarity is a powerful motivator. The status quo, no matter how objectionable, appears to many as the only possible reality. Adams defeated familiarity with logic, revealing the familiar situation as irrational and, therefore, no longer tolerable. An effective leader leads the organization toward the best possible reality, even if this means, through reasoned revelation, blowing up the currently prevailing reality.

**Lesson 11**

## SOMETIMES THE BEST OFFENSE IS A GOOD DEFENSE

*The patriots of this province desire nothing new; they wish only to keep their old privileges.*

—*Novanglus*, 1774–1775

Adams was at pains to define the American Revolution as a war of defense, a struggle not to win something new, but to recover something usurped: a set of rights. The patriots, he wrote, "were, for one hundred and fifty years, allowed to tax themselves, and govern their internal concerns as they thought best." Parliament having moved to deprive them of these rights, the patriots had no choice but to defend them. Indeed, it was the actions of Parliament, not of the patriots, that escalated this defensive action into a full-scale revolution. As long as taxation and internal administration rested in colonial hands, the colonists were content to allow Parliament to govern "their trade as they [Parliament] saw fit. This plan they [the colonists] wish may continue forever." Nevertheless, "rather than become subject to the absolute authority of parliament in all cases of taxation and internal polity, they will be driven to throw off that of regulating trade" as well.

**The Last Word:** Sometimes the most effective means of motivating action is not to tempt people with what they may gain by taking action, but to apprise them of what they stand to lose by failing to act. Most people dread loss far more strongly than they covet gain. A skilled manager knows when to accent the positive as well as when to play up the negative.

**Lesson 12**

AUTHORITY AND ACCIDENT

*It is true . . . "that the bulk of the people are generally but little versed in the affairs of state;". . . they "rest the affairs of government in the hands where accident has placed them."*

—*Novanglus,* 1774–1775

To a sometimes astounding degree, people are content to be ruled by accidental authority, resting "the affairs of government in the hands where accident has placed them." Adams found his greatest enemy not in the British Crown or Parliament, but in the complacency of so many of his own countrymen. In this, he shared the lot common to all leaders of change: the great fact of inertia and the necessity of overcoming it. Step one is persuading others that the status quo is unsatisfactory or destructive. Step two is persuading them that the status quo may be largely a result of accident and, as such, hardly a permanent fixture in the scheme of things.

The Last Word: Managing for change requires persuading others that change is both necessary and possible.

## Lesson 13
## Command the Facts

*[L]et ... any ... confute me.*

—*Novanglus*, 1774–1775

Britain's prime minister and chancellor of the exchequer Lord North sought to justify the taxes levied on the colonies by calling them measures intended to get the Americans to pay some share of the costs of "the empire," including the costs of defense. Loyalists in America, including "Massachusettensis," author of a Loyalist pamphlet Adams refuted in his "Novanglus" essays, echoed this rationale. Adams responded with a challenge to "Massachusettensis or any other friend of the minister [Lord North] to confute me," and backed that challenge by impressively marshalling facts to demonstrate that, when properly accounted for, it was clear that the American colonies paid even more than their fair share of the empire's expenses. Laws obliging the colonies "to take from Great Britain commodities that we could purchase cheaper elsewhere," combined with laws restricting colonial exports exclusively to Great Britain, effectively resulted in a tax greater than those paid by any three million people (the population of the American colonies at the time) in any other part of Great Britain. "All this may be computed and reduced to stubborn figures by the minister, if he pleases," Adams wrote. "We cannot do it; we have not the accounts, records, &c. Now let this account be fairly stated, and I will engage for America, upon any penalty, that she will pay the overplus, if any."

**The Last Word:** Facts are tough soldiers. Recruit them, organize them, send them into battle.

**Lesson 14**

NEGOTIATE FOR HEARTS AND MINDS

*I thought it our duty . . . to say every thing we could to the Englishmen here, in order that just sentiments might prevail in England at this moment.*

—Diary, October 20, 1782

Adams's strategy for negotiating the treaty that would end the American Revolution was not simply to present the demands of the United States, but to win the hearts and minds of the English treaty commissioners and government, "to countenance every man well-disposed" to the United States and "to disabuse and undeceive everybody" else. He believed that the negotiation was "a crisis in which good will or ill will towards America would be carried very far in England," and he saw his job as "turning the tide" of English sentiment toward a generous treaty granting full independence. If necessary, he was resolved to use his influence to influence "changes of administration" in the British government.

**The Last Word:** Negotiation is not about winning by defeating your opposite number, but is all about creating the intellectual and emotional conditions that will enable the other party to give you what you want. Each successful negotiation is, in effect, a work of public relations, the creation of a new reality that is favorable to you and your goals.

**Lesson 15**

## A "Passion for Distinction"

*A desire to be observed, considered, esteemed, praised, beloved, and admired by his fellows, is one of the earliest, as well as keenest dispositions discovered in the heart of man.*

—*Discourses on Davila*, 1790–1791

John Adams was a lawyer by training and by trade, but he was a psychologist by inclination. Endlessly fascinated by human behavior, he was firmly convinced that people were driven by what he termed natural passions, among which was a "passion for distinction," an irresistible drive to "be observed, considered, esteemed, praised, beloved" by one's "fellows." This passion was a force in human affairs and, like all forces, was in itself morally neutral, capable of driving people to good as well as ill, to constructive ends as well as destructive ones. The key—again, as with all forces—was control.

**The Last Word:** Recognize the passion for distinction. School yourself in the art of harnessing this passion. Uncontrolled, it leads to an egocentric orientation and a heedless will to outshine others, to scorn team effort, to climb the corporate ladder (or its equivalent) with little or no regard for the common good of an organization. Properly managed, however, the passion is essential to creating excellence by encouraging original thought and maximum effort.

**Lesson 16**

## John Adams's Motivational Secrets

*The desire of the esteem of others is as real a want of nature as hunger; and the neglect and contempt of the world as severe a pain as the gout or stone.*

—*Discourses on Davila,* 1790–1791

As a designer of government, John Adams was no mere theorist. He delved deeply into the roots of human behavior, especially the topic of motivation: incentive and disincentive.

It is not surprising that one of his closest friends was Dr. Benjamin Rush, the Philadelphia physician who is often called the father of American psychiatry. Adams and Rush must frequently have discussed psychology, and certainly Adams thought deeply about it.

Adams believed that human beings, even in a primitive state, were ceaselessly driven to be noticed by others. As society became more sophisticated, they hungered after a specific form of notice, *esteem,* and, conversely, they dreaded both "neglect" (the opposite of notice) and "contempt" (the opposite of esteem).

Adams developed this basic psychological scheme yet further. "Every man not only desires the consideration of others," he wrote, "but he frequently compares himself with others . . . and in proportion as he exults when he perceives that he has more of it [that is, more of the consideration of others] than they, he feels a keener affliction when he sees that one or more of them, are more respected than himself." Adams wrote that "this passion," when it is "simply a desire to excel another, by fair industry in search of truth, and the practice of virtue, is properly called *Emulation.*" But, he continued, when the passion "aims at power, as a means of distinction, it is *Ambition.*" This same passion, "in a situation to suggest the sentiments of fear and apprehension, that another, who is now inferior, will become superior," becomes "*Jealousy.*" This he distinguished from "*Envy,*" which is the operation of the passion for notice "in a state of mortification, at the superiority of another, and desires to bring him down to our level, or to depress him below us."

There was yet more. "When it [the passion for notice] deceives a man into a belief of false professions of esteem or admiration, or into a false opinion of his importance in the judgment of the world, it is *Vanity.*"

This well-developed psychology was typical of Adams's view of reality. His was a universe of forces—in human beings these forces were usually called "passions"—which were commodities neither good nor bad in themselves, but rendered one or the other by how they were regulated, suppressed, expressed, and generally managed. The force, the passion, for notice became in civilized society a drive to gain esteem and to avoid contempt. The skilled leader appealed to and manipulated this universal passion to achieve constructive ends that contribute to the advancement of the enterprise—whether this was a company or a nation. The leader cannot instill the passion in people. It is a force, a natural energy that can neither be created nor destroyed. But the leader must shape, control, use, and manage that passion, preventing it from taking on negative and destructive forms such as jealousy, envy, and vanity—or wholly self-centered ambition—and channeling into productive emulation and a desire to earn the esteem of others.

**The Last Word:** All great organizations, no matter how vast, are built on and nurtured by the skillfully managed passion of their members.

**Lesson 17**

AN IRRESISTIBLE DELUSION

*Fame . . . There is no greater possible or imaginable delusion. Yet the impulse is irresistible.*

—*Discourses on Davila,* 1790–1791

"What is it to us what shall be said of us after we are dead?" Adams asked. "Or in Asia, Africa, or Europe, while we live?" Fame is nothing but a "fancied life in others' breath," and, as such, a stupendous "delusion." Does this mean that it should be scorned and rejected as a motive and a motivator? Adams's answer: absolutely not. Although fame was a great delusion, the impulse to achieve it was nevertheless irresistible. For that very reason, fame was immensely valuable as a motivator, a mover of action. Delusion or not, fame was a force, literally and figuratively a *motive force,* and, like any other source of energy, it was not a commodity to be overlooked or squandered, but rather harnessed, regulated, and used.

**The Last Word:** To lead others, use whatever sources of power you have. The most effective are those that come from within rather than those applied from without. The drive to gain notice—to earn fame—is part of human nature, and the leader who taps into it and engages it wields a strong motivator, whether he believes wholeheartedly in it—or not at all.

**Lesson 18**

# THE ECONOMICS OF MOTIVATION

*Glory ... Man constantly craves for more, even when he has no rival.*
—*Discourses on Davila*, 1790–1791

Economics is a complex subject, but the foundation of the modern science is very simple: Desires are limitless, but resources are limited—or, as economists put it, scarce. So it was, according to Adams, with glory. Man constantly craved for more, yet the sources of it were limited—or, at least, insufficient to satisfy an infinite craving. In this, the passion for glory was "like all other human desires, unlimited and insatiable."

Depending on how one looks at this, the human condition, effective leadership is either impossible or eminently feasible. If you conceive the manager's role as satisfying everyone's desire for glory, you are doomed to fail. "Like all other human desires," the desire for glory is "unlimited and insatiable." If, however, you see management as drawing on, exploiting, shaping, and directing the common human desire for glory—for achievement, for approval, for applause, for reward—then the management task becomes quite doable, precisely because you have an unlimited fund of desire on which to draw.

The Last Word: Leadership is less about satisfying human desire than it is about using—managing—it effectively, toward productive goals that perpetuate, develop, and grow the enterprise.

**Lesson 19**

## THE MONEY MOTIVE

*Why do men pursue riches?*

—*Discourses on Davila*, 1790–1791

"The labor and anxiety . . . that are voluntarily undertaken in pursuit of gain," Adams wrote, "are out of all proportion to the utility, convenience, or pleasure of riches. A competence [that is, a sufficient income] to satisfy the wants of nature, food and clothes, a shelter from the seasons, and the comforts of a family, may be had for very little. . . . For what reason, then, are any mortals averse to the situation of the farmer, mechanic, or laborer? Why do we tempt the seas and encompass the globe? Why do any men affront heaven and earth to accumulate wealth . . . ? What connection can there be between wealth and pride?"

Why, Adams asked, was money so strong a motive in so many human endeavors?

He had an answer: "*[B]ecause riches attract the attention, consideration, and congratulations of mankind.*"

People do not risk and sacrifice for the elusive purpose of gaining "more ease or pleasure than the poor," but, rather, because "[r]iches force the opinion on a man that he is the object of the congratulations of others." Wealth attracts attention—positive attention, in the form of "congratulations"—and that, rather than the money itself, is what humanity universally craves. So much so that, though his "conscience is clear," the poor man is nevertheless "ashamed," and while his "character is irreproachable," he is nevertheless "neglected and despised. He feels himself out of the sight of others, groping in the dark." As a sense of positive attention—of congratulations—satisfies a hunger, so the sense of neglect inflicts an acute pain.

**The Last Word:** It comes as a surprise to no manager that money is a powerful incentive. The people you lead will work all the harder for the prospect of a raise or promotion. In the carrot-and-stick arsenal of motivators, money may be the most delicious carrot of all. And yet it is a mistake to reduce all motivation to money, especially since money is not an absolute end in itself. Whatever comfort and security money buys, it may function even more compellingly as a symbol of success, a means of attracting the "congratulations" of others. Money, as such, has its limits as a motivator. As a symbol of greater achievement, however, money lies at the very heart of motivation in its near association with a basic human drive for recognition. Never reduce motivation to a game of mere numbers. The truth be known, nobody, no matter how sophisticated, really wants to be cynical about money.

**Lesson 20**

*MERE* TOKENS?

---

*What is it that bewitches mankind to marks and signs?*
—*Discourses on Davila*, 1790–1791

"A ribbon? a garter? a star? a golden key? a marshal's staff? . . . Though there is in such frivolities as these neither profit nor pleasure, nor any thing amiable, estimable, or respectable, yet experience teaches us, in every country of the world, they attract the attention of mankind more than parts of learning, virtue or religion. They are, therefore, sought with ardor."

Many political philosophers would scoff at "ardor" for a "ribbon." Adams surely understood the nature of ardor and the insubstantiality of a ribbon. But he did not scoff. Instead, he saw such symbols as an appeal to the senses, which constituted "the direct road to" the "passions." And the passions were the driving force of all achievement. For proof of this, he looked to ancient Rome, where "Roman wisdom" employed "the language of signs . . . to excite the emulation and active virtue of the citizens." Each rank had its exclusive emblem—the purple-studded laticlave robe worn by kings and then by senators, the smaller augusticlave worn by "Roman knights," the "praetext, or long white robe . . . worn by the principal magistrates," and a panoply of other symbols, emblems, and ornaments, each "addressed to the emulation of the citizens," each "calculated to attract the attention, to allure the consideration and excite the congratulations of the people; to attach their hearts to individual citizens according to their merit." And such use of the "language of signs" was "in the true spirit of republics, in which form of government there is no other consistent method of preserving order, or procuring submission to the laws."

*Revolutionary Wisdom*
"I seem to have lost sight of the object that I resolved to pursue. Dreams and slumbers, sloth and negligence, will be the ruin of my schemes. However, I seem to be awake now; why can't I keep awake? I have wrote Scripture pretty industriously this morning. Why am I so unreasonable as to expect happiness, and a solid, undisturbed contentment, amidst all the disorders and the continual rotations of worldly affairs?"

—*Diary, July 14, 1756*

**The Last Word:** Ribbons are cloth. Transform them into symbols, and they excite the passions, creating strong motivation for whatever purposes the society, the nation, or any other worthwhile enterprise has assigned. Adams understood that ornaments and tokens had no intrinsic value, but that they could be endowed with almost incalculable value as potent instigators of action. No leader can ignore them, disdain them, or, worst of all, treat them cynically. They carry meaning, they focus effort, and they command loyalty.

**Lesson 21**

## The Limits of Patriotism

*Is it to be supposed that the regular standing armies of Europe engage in the service from pure motives of patriotism?*

—*Discourses on Davila*, 1790–1791

What, Adams asked, drives men to "risk their lives and reconcile themselves to wounds" in military service? A sense of "moral or religious duty"? "Pure motives of patriotism"? The expectation of "reward in a future life"? As with other modes of sacrifice, Adams believed he had an answer. They are motivated by "the consideration and chances of laurels which they acquire by the service." The private "contends for promotion to be a corporal. The corporals vie with each other to be sergeants" and so on, "every man . . . constantly aspiring to be something higher." It is no different in the army than in civilian life, in which "every citizen . . . is constantly struggling for a better rank, that he may draw the observation of more eyes."

Managers tend to believe that their staff members aspire to greater authority and responsibility for the sake of earning more money and rising within their profession. Doubtless there is truth in this, and John Adams would have conceded it. Nevertheless, the underlying—and probably stronger—source of motivation is a common human drive to "draw the observation of more eyes."

*Revolutionary Wisdom*

"Whenever I arrive at any port in Europe, whether in Spain or France, my first inquiry should be concerning the designs of the enemy. What force they mean to send to America? where they are to obtain men? what is the state of the British nation? what the state of parties? What the state of finances and of stocks? Then the state of Europe, particularly France and Spain. What the real design of those courts? What the conditions of their finances? what the state of their armies, but especially, of their fleets? what number of ships, they have fitted for this seat? what their names, number of men and guns, weight of metal, &c., where they lie, &c. the probability or improbability of a war, and the causes and reasons for and against each supposition. The supplies and clothing, arms, &c., gone to America during the past winter. The state of American credit in France. What remittances have been made from America and tobacco, rights, indigo, or any other articles?"

—*Diary, while en route to France, March 5, 1778*

**The Last Word:** Loyalty in corporate affairs, like patriotism in national affairs, goes only so far. It is the most admirable motive, yet just because it is the most admirable does not make it the most likely motive. Look beneath loyalty and patriotism, and you may well find a hunger for recognition. The idealistic leader is tempted to shrink from this and to reject such a motive. The pragmatic leader, however, embraces it, builds on it, and if others wish to call it patriotism or loyalty, he will call it that, too.

**Lesson 22**

ON SACRIFICE

---

*Is there in science and letters a reward for the labor they require?*
—*Discourses on Davila*, 1790–1791

How real, Adams asked, is selflessness? Consider the scientist or scholar. "Scholars learn the dead languages of antiquity, as well as the living tongues of modern nations; those of the east, as well as the west. They puzzle themselves and others with metaphysics and mathematics. They renounce their pleasures, neglect their exercises, and destroy their health, for what? Is curiosity so strong? Is the pleasure that accompanies the pursuit and acquisition of knowledge so exquisite?"

Maybe.

"A sense of duty," Adams conceded, "a love of truth; a desire to alleviate the anxieties of ignorance, may, no doubt, have an influence on some minds." Yet these motives seemed weak to him. He had to look elsewhere for "the universal object and idol of men of letters." He found it in "*reputation*. It is the *notoriety*, the *celebration*, which constitutes the charm that is to compensate the loss of appetite and sleep, and sometimes riches and honors."

Most sacrifice is really *apparent* sacrifice, sacrifice for gain— for the satisfaction of the universal human craving after reputation, notoriety, celebration. Leaders must, from time to time, ask others to make sacrifices. To the degree that the sacrifice is viewed strictly as a sacrifice, a relinquishment and loss, the leader's work of persuasion is made difficult. Frame that sacrifice as an opportunity to earn reputation, notoriety, and celebration, and it comes to seem a gain, something of great worth.

*Revolutionary Wisdom*

"Dr. Franklin, one of my colleagues, is so generally known that I shall not attempt a sketch of his character at present. That he was a great genius, a great wit, a great humorist, a great satirist, and a great politician, is certain. That he was a great philosopher, a great moralist, and a great statesman, is more questionable."

—*Manuscript autobiography, referring to Benjamin Franklin in Paris, 1778*

**The Last Word:** The leader who can shape sacrifice in this manner is powerfully persuasive. Lincoln did it. Roosevelt did it. Kennedy did it. Washington the general surely did it, and, in his best moments, John Adams did it.

**Lesson 23**

## THE ROMAN WAY

*Has there ever been a nation who understood the human heart better than the Romans, or made better use of the passion for consideration, congratulation, and distinction?*

—*Discourses on Davila,* 1790–1791

The Roman republic, more than the democratic ideals of the earlier Greek philosophers, served the founding fathers as an inspiration, guide, and model in creating the American government. Like most of his fellow thinkers and politicians, John Adams was steeped in the classics, but whereas others concentrated specifically on traditions of Roman law, Adams focused on Roman motivational psychology. He believed that the greatness of Roman republican government flowed from an understanding of the human heart and a willingness to build the government upon this understanding. In particular, Roman society was defined by the constructive "use" of what Adams defined as an essential human drive, the hunger—for it was a hunger, as surely as a hunger for sustenance—to be noticed, "the passion for consideration, congratulation, and distinction." Whereas some societies have allowed this passion to run wild and others have attempted to suppress it as unseemly or even dangerous, the Romans harnessed it, mastered it, seized control of it, and shaped it. They built their republican government as a hierarchy of offices, each distinguished not by a particular level of authority alone, but also by certain exclusive symbolic trappings—robes, batons, jewels, and the like. Each station in society and government was made to appeal to the senses. Each station was made to seem desirable and worth sacrificing for. Each was made to seem a step leading to the next. Adams hoped that his countrymen would learn from this method of "preserving order" and "procuring submission to laws."

**The Last Word:** There is a management style that disdains distinctions and hierarchies. Indeed, we are told, the prevailing model for most corporate organizations has become flat, with teams and work groups supplanting the old hierarchies of workers, supervisors, field managers, and top managers, or executives. The example of Rome—and of John Adams's understanding of Rome—should give us pause to think before we pound any organization into total flatness. Teams and work groups can be effective, but there is also a utility in hierarchy, provided that movement within that hierarchy is not only possible, but expected. A stepwise rise through the organization may be more than a corporate convention. The Romans believed it was ingrained in the human heart, and they modeled their national enterprise in its image. Adams, for one, believed they had something there.

## Lesson 24
## "MELANCHOLY AND ALARMING"

*I must own to you that the daring Traits of Ambition and Intrigue, and those unbridled Rivalries which have already appeared, are the most melancholy and alarming Symptoms that I have ever seen in this Country.*
—Letter to Thomas Jefferson, July 29, 1791

Ambition, intrigue, and infighting—rivalries—were, as Adams saw it, incompatible with patriotism and therefore destructive to government and the nation. Yet anyone who has ever led or managed any organization must recognize that ambition, intrigue, and infighting are to be expected whenever a business grows beyond a single person. Doubtless, Adams—the ultimate and always unblinking realist when it came to organizational behavior—understood this as well. He was a very careful, very precise writer, and so we must look closely at exactly what he wrote to Jefferson.

Look closely at his words. The problem was not simply ambition and intrigue, but these qualities in the form of "*daring* Traits." And it was not rivalries per se that worried him, but "*unbridled* Rivalries."

Ambition, intrigue, rivalry—these are realities, and they are also the individual engines that drive organizations. It would be both undesirable and (in any case) impossible to extinguish these realities. Adams therefore proposed no such thing. The danger lay in their being "daring" and "unbridled." Like any other passion, these human traits are forces to be managed, to be used productively, to be transformed from "daring" to "creative." To be "bridled"—harnessed, rendered controllable and therefore useful.

*Revolutionary Wisdom*
"By my physical constitution, I am but an ordinary man. The times alone have destined me to fame; and even these have not been able to give me much."

—*Diary, February 26, 1779*

**The Last Word:** An effective manager does not avoid, evade, deny, or seek to extinguish impolite or even downright unseemly traits, either in herself or in those who work for her. Instead, she finds ways to use them, to "bridle" them, to make them creative. She finds strategies that persuade everyone to subordinate their drives to the common good. But that does not mean she attempts to deny internal competition. For, in many cases, competition, ambition, intrigue, and rivalry are precisely what is needed to advance the enterprise. The engine that propels the fastest sports car is driven by forceful compression and violent explosion, not the gentle and harmonious music of the spheres.

**Lesson 25**
PROBABLE IMPROVABILITY

*For I am a Believer, in the probable improvability and Improvement, the Ameliorabi[li]ty and Amelioration in human Affairs: though I never could understand the Doctrine of the Perfectibility of the human Mind.*
—Letter to Thomas Jefferson, July 16, 1813

Few thinkers have had such profound influence on the course of history than the eighteenth-century French philosopher Jean-Jacques Rousseau, one of the leading advocates of the doctrine of the "perfectibility of man," the idea that human beings have the capacity to achieve perfection on earth through natural means and without the grace of God. Thomas Jefferson was a believer, and he saw the American Revolution as well as the establishment of democratic government as steps toward implementing this perfectibility. John Adams, in contrast, found the notion of human perfectibility simply beyond understanding, an instance of mysticism requiring a suspension of rational thought. Yet his rejection of perfectibility as a reasonable *end* of human endeavor did not require rejecting the *means* Jefferson and others proposed for reaching that end. If Adams could not believe in perfectibility, he earnestly believed in "improvability," and the means toward that end, he recognized, were not much different from those proposed to reach perfectibility. Both goals, after all, lay in the same direction.

*Revolutionary Wisdom*

"Whenever I sett down to write to you, I am precisely in the Situation of the Wood Cutter on Mount Ida: I can not see Wood for Trees. So many Subjects crowd upon me that I know not, with which to begin."

—*Letter to Thomas Jefferson, July 9, 1813*

**The Last Word:** Many managers regard "compromise" as a dirty word. In fact, it is an essential management tool. Those leaders who set the bar of achievement the highest set perfection as their goal. There is nothing wrong with this, provided that perfection is recognized as neither more nor less than a compelling symbol, a powerful myth, rather than as a practical end. If the hypothesis of perfectibility drives you and your organization to excellence, keep it and use it. Just don't sacrifice improvability to it. In the real world, the best really is the enemy of the good. Do set the loftiest standards and goals possible, but celebrate those occasions when you approach them, closer and closer, even as you fall short of them time after time.

## Lesson 26
## What's in a Name?

*Have names no influence in governing men? . . . Have the words "Ja-cobin," "democrat," no influence? Have the words "federalist" and "repub-lican" no effect?*

—Letter to John Taylor, April 15, 1814

Shakespeare asked "What's in a name?" and answered that, whatever you choose to call a rose, it will smell as sweet nevertheless. Adams did not argue with the Bard, but he did believe in the power of names to influence governments and people. Labels affect perception, often unreasonably so. Adams believed, for example, that the word "democracy" cast a spell that caused many to regard uncritically any government or proposal for government that called itself democratic.

Yet while it is dangerous to mistake mere labels for reality, it is equally hazardous to discount the power of labels.

John Adams was no modern relativist. He believed in absolute reality and absolute morality. Nevertheless, he counted perception as an aspect of reality, and he understood that naming something was often as much an act of creation as it was of description.

### Revolutionary Wisdom

"Every nobleman envies his sovereign, and would pull him down, if he could get into his throne and wear his crown. But when nobles and ignobles have torn one another to pieces for years or ages in their eternal squabbles of jealousy, envy, rivalry, hatred, and revenge, and all are convinced that this anarchy will not do, that the world will be depopulated, that a head must be set up, and all the members must be guided by it, then, and not till then, will nobles submit to Kings as of superior birth. What subjects all the nobility of Europe to all the kings of Europe, but birth?"

—*Letter to John Taylor, April 15, 1814*

**The Last Word:** You need to consider carefully what you call something or someone. Calling a problem a "problem" is likely to prompt a certain approach and a certain result that will differ from what happens when you call that same thing a "challenge" or an "opportunity." Creating productive perceptions is a key management task, and supplying the names for concepts, commodities, objectives, and goals of concern to the enterprise is the royal road to creating the perceptions you want and need.

Lesson 27
OUT OF TOUCH

*They seemed to believe, that whole Nations and Continents had been changed in their Principles Opinions Habits and Feelings by the Sovereign Grace of their Almighty Philosophy.*

—Letter to Thomas Jefferson, March 2, 1816

"No man is more Sensible than I am, of the Service to Science and Letters, Humanity, Fraternity, and Liberty, that would have been rendered by the [French] Encyclopedists and Economists, By Voltaire, Dalembert, Buffon[,] Diderot, Rousseau[,] La Lande, Frederick [the Great] and Catharine [the Great], if they had possessed Common Sense. But they were all totally destitute of it." The greatest thinkers and leaders of state during the age that created the French Revolution and that influenced the American republic were, Adams admitted, geniuses, but they failed to be genuinely, practically, and enduringly useful to civilization because they lacked common sense. Had they possessed it, they would have shed their hubris and would therefore not have believed "that whole Nations and Continents had been changed in their Principles Opinions Habits and Feelings by the Sovereign Grace of their Almighty Philosophy, almost as suddenly as Catholicks and Calvin[ists] believe in instantaneous [religious] Conversion." Lacking common sense, however, this train of geniuses had failed to take into account "the force of early Education on the Millions of Minds who had never heard of their Philosophy."

It is possible, all too possible, Adams realized, even for a genius to be out of touch with the world. Those who make bold to think in new directions, to design new governments or to create new sciences, dare to make an impact on reality. Those who actually succeed in making such an impact, do not, however, ignore reality. They engage it. They get in touch with it. Common sense compels them to.

**The Last Word:** Even the most original and innovative leader must remain in contact with reality as it is. It is not an object fit only for contempt. On the contrary, it is the very medium that must be managed and massaged into new shapes. Being in touch with the realities of your business, of the marketplace, of your customers, of the state of the art, and of the needs, abilities, and desires of your subordinates, your superiors, and your peers does not shackle innovation, but inspires it. Even more important, this grounding in reality enables the implementation of innovation. Audacity can be a powerful engine of achievement, but hubris leads nowhere—or, at least, nowhere you want to go.

# CHAPTER 3

# *Regulation*

## Lesson 28
### PERFECTION OR MADNESS?

---

*No man is entirely free from weakness and imperfection in this life. Men of the most exalted genius and active minds are generally most perfect slaves to the love of fame. . . . The greatest men have been the most envious, malicious, and vengeful. . . . The ambitious man rolls and tumbles in his bed, a stranger to refreshing sleep and repose, through anxiety about a preferment he has in view. The philosopher sweats and labors at his book, and ruminates in his closet, till his bearded and grim countenance exhibits effigies of pale want and care and death . . . Is this perfection, or downright madness and distraction?*

—Diary, February 19, 1756

The Puritan forebears of John Adams were steeped in a theology of original sin, the doctrine that humanity was by its nature wicked. Adams did not share this belief, but he was nevertheless deeply affected by it. Human beings, he knew, were capable of greatness, yet even the great were weak, for it was weakness and imperfection that constituted the lot of humankind. These afflictions were as natural to men and women as the possession of two arms and two legs. Weakness and imperfection were species specific. There was no freedom from these defects—but they could be managed.

Absorption in any cause, motive, passion, or talent was, as Adams saw it, a manifestation of imperfection and weakness. What the mass of people called greatness—"exalted genius," say, or intense philosophical devotion—was as dangerous as any other extreme. For Adams, greatness, like any other force, required wary management to moderate it, to integrate it among other human qualities, and to direct it toward useful, ethical, balanced ends.

*Revolutionary Wisdom*

"Human Nature, in no form of it, ever could bear Prosperity. That peculiar tribe of Men, called Conquerors, more remarkably than any other have been swelled with Vanity by any Series of Victories. Napoleon won so many mighty Battles in such quick succession and for so long a time, that it was no wonder his brain became completely intoxicated and his enterprises, rash, extravagant and mad."

—*Letter to Thomas Jefferson, July 16, 1814*

**The Last Word:** Nothing partial—nothing too intensely concentrated, too narrowly focused—can be deemed "perfection," which, by definition, must be balanced, even holistic. Blind passion, unheeding reason, an unchecked hunger for fame, all of these, though qualities of men and women many call great, lead to "downright madness and distraction."

**Lesson 29**

## KNOW THE LIMIT OF KNOWING

*We, who see but a few cogs in one wheel of the great machine of the universe, can make no right judgment of particular phenomena of nature.*
—Diary, May 4, 1756

John Adams devoted much of his life to the law, which he saw as the necessary imposition of general principle upon the particular realities of life, yet he never allowed himself to become absorbed in or lost among sheer abstractions. For Adams, the loftiest principles were always grounded in everyday reality. He mused in his diary over the prospect of "any man . . . of the most improved understanding" examining "a watch when the parts are separated. Let him examine every wheel and spring separately by itself. Yet, if the use and application of these springs and wheels is not explained to him, he will not be able to judge of the use and advantage of particular parts; much less will he be able if he has only one wheel."

So it is with our understanding of the universe, Adams wrote. Doomed to see but some small parts of it, separated from the whole, our knowledge is necessarily limited.

The implications of this insight are many. With regard to religion, it suggests that much must be taken on faith. With regard to any large, complex system—whether the universe, a nation, or any vast organization—it defines the limits of individual perspective and understanding, and it implies that the more narrowly local or partial a manager's perspective, the less effective he will be; conversely, the greater the effort a leader makes to see parts in the context of the whole, the more effective he will be. But it is no easy assignment to understand the local yet possess the ability to look beyond it in order to build global understanding, knowledge of the whole. This early leadership insight of John Adams acknowledges the necessity of integrating knowledge of parts into a thorough concept of the whole and yet recognizes as well the difficulty of doing this most necessary of perceptual and intellectual tasks.

*Revolutionary Wisdom*

"All Nations, known in History or in Travels have hoped, believed, and expected a future and a better State. The Maker of the Universe, the Cause of all Things, whether We call it, *Fate* or *Chance* or GOD has inspired this Hope. If it is a *Fraud*, We shall never know it. We shall never resent the Imposition, be grateful for the Illusion, nor grieve for the disappointment. We shall be no more."

—*Letter to Thomas Jefferson, May 3, 1816*

**The Last Word:** Vision, in the fullest sense of the word, is vital to leadership.

## Lesson 30
## SELF-DECEIT

*There is nothing in the science of human nature more curious, or that deserves a critical attention from every order of men so much, as that principle which moral writers have distinguished by the name of self-deceit.*
—"On Self-Delusion," *Boston Gazette,* August 1763

The ancestors of John Adams in America were Puritans, believers in original sin, a doctrine of the inherently impure state of humankind. Adams did not believe people were inherently sinful or evil, but he did find in humanity a staggering capacity for self-delusion and self-deceit, sometimes a helpless lack of self awareness and at times a willful ignorance. Had he been a Puritan in the mold of his forbears, Adams would have despaired of republican government and participatory democracy. To bring many together in order to govern themselves would be doing nothing more than pooling ignorance, creating a collective body of self-deceit. Instead, in participatory government, Adams saw an antidote to self-deceit. The vigilance of a government truly of and by the people would not reinforce or multiply self-delusion, but would be a check, a balance, and a corrective on it. "Every step in the public administration of government," he pointed out, "concerns us nearly. Life and fortune, our own and those of our posterity, are not trifles to be neglected or totally entrusted to other hands."

**The Last Word:** The real strength of any organization is not derived from a monolithic, dictatorial system of management, but from the management of a multiplicity of perspectives, some more useful than others, but all valuable.

## Lesson 31
## Law as Portal, Law as Wall

*Numberless have been the systems of iniquity contrived by the great for the gratification of this passion [for dominance] . . . but in none of them were they ever more successful than in the invention and establishment of the canon and the feudal law.*

—*A Dissertation on the Canon and Feudal Law*, 1765

His father wanted him to become a minister, but John Adams turned instead to the law, which, for him, was a kind of religion. It existed to govern and restrain the passions and forces that drive humankind. It existed to elevate government and civilization above any one man or group of men whose unrestrained power might lead them to become tyrants by sheer force. In this sense, the law served as a portal to right, justice, and liberty, unchanging principles that "cannot be repealed or restrained." Yet it was also clearly possible to pervert the law, to make of it not a portal admitting access to right, justice, and liberty, but a wall that barred that access.

Adams argued that the Catholic Church, historically, had erected just such a wall from the body of canon law, and that the rulers of medieval Europe did so from the feudal law. These "systems of iniquity" stood between the people and their rights—between the people and the truth—by "reducing their minds to a state of sordid ignorance and staring timidity" in large part by "infusing into them a religious horror of letters and knowledge."

Adams defined ignorance as a severance from the truth, which included right, justice, and liberty. People in a state of ignorance mistook either their own passions for ultimate reality or the reality supplied to them by Church and feudal lord: the body of doctrine Adams called the canon and the feudal law. The first step in any great social change was education, the banishment of ignorance for the purpose of connecting people with what had always been theirs, though unknown to them: right, liberty, justice.

**The Last Word:** Leadership requires rules, policies, and laws. Good leadership, leadership designed to build enduring organizations and worthwhile enterprises, requires rules, policies, and laws that connect with reality in genuinely productive and ethical ways, that guide and make possible actions and behavior likely to contribute to the prosperity of the common endeavor.

**Lesson 32**

## Parental Government

*Is there not something extremely fallacious in the common-place images of mother country and children colonies?*

*—A Dissertation on the Canon and Feudal Law, 1765*

In opposing the infamous Stamp Act of 1765, John Adams attacked, among other ideas, the concept that "Britain is the mother and we the children" and that, therefore, "a filial duty and submission is due from us to her." It was a model of government widespread on both sides of the Atlantic, and many allowed it to define their understanding of relations between the colonies and Britain. Adams, however, saw it for what it was: a destructive analogy and a dangerous fiction. He asked his readers: "Are we the children of Great Britain any more than the cities of London, Exeter, and Bath? Are we not brethren and fellow subjects with those in Britain, only under a somewhat different method of legislation, and a totally different method of taxation?" And in a brilliant argumentative stroke, he turned the analogy against those who offered it: "But admitting we are children, have not children a right to complain when their parents are attempting to break their limbs, to administer poison, to sell them to enemies for slaves?" We are not the children of the Crown, Adams argued, but, even if we were, have we not the right to complain about a lethal mother, one who is "deaf to the cries of her children"?

In the late 1960s, a school of psychotherapy emerged known as Transactional Analysis. It was based on the assumption that people tend to relate to one another according to paradigms that are dominated by one of three aspects of their personality, a parent aspect, a child aspect, and an adult aspect. Too often, relationships become dysfunctional because two adults relate to one another as parent and child rather than adult and adult. In 1756, Adams saw a similar dysfunction in the child-mother country paradigm that, for all too many, defined American-British relations.

**The Last Word:** Management based on a literal extension of the family paradigm is doomed to fail because no serious, competitive enterprise can productively exist staffed by adults who define themselves as children. Conversely, employees who look upon their manager as a father or mother are bound to be disappointed, dismayed, and misguided. Management, like government, must be a transaction among equals, all adults, no parents or children allowed.

**Lesson 33**

## Passing the Test of Common Sense

*They knew that government was a plain, simple, intelligible thing, founded in nature and reason, and quite comprehensible by common sense.*
— *A Dissertation on the Canon an115d Feudal Law*, 1765

One of the things for which Adams most admired his Puritan ancestors was their conception of government as "a plain, simple, intelligible thing . . . quite comprehensible by common sense." Expressed in
1765, this became for Adams the test of all proposed aspects of government. Through the Revolution, the creation of the Constitution,
and his presidency, he asked of each proposed concept or law: *Is this
principle "founded in nature and reason"?* And this question implied
another: *Is this "comprehensible by common sense"?* If something can
be apprehended by common sense, it almost certainly is founded in
nature and reason.

**The Last Word:** Whatever else they accomplish, laws, rules,
policies, and directives should make sense and should, therefore,
appeal to the common sense. It is an infallible litmus test.

**Lesson 34**
## Protection from the Weak or Wicked

*What can be wanting . . . but a weak or wicked man for a judge, to render us the most sordid and forlorn of slaves?—we mean the slaves of a slave of the servants of a minister of state.*
—"Instructions of the Town of Braintree to Their Representative," 1765

As if the taxes imposed by the Stamp Act were not sufficiently galling to the colonists, the legislation was made more repugnant by what Adams characterized as "the most grievous innovation of all, . . . the alarming extension of the power of the courts of admiralty." Constituted by the Crown, not by the people of the colonies, the courts of admiralty were empowered to decide all cases brought under the Stamp Act. "In these courts," Adams exclaimed, "one judge presides alone! No juries have any concern there! The law and the fact are both to be decided by the same single judge," who acted not by colonial authority, but "independent of every power on earth,— independent of the King, the Lords, the Commons, the people." Nevertheless, a judge's continuation in his commission depended on relations between Crown and colony remaining unchanged. The power of a crown judge was, in effect, limitless, without regulation. It was certainly possible, by some good fortune, that a particular judge might indeed be a fine and honorable man, but what if a "weak or wicked man" became a judge, one who thought only about maintaining the status quo, which is to say thought only about his own self-interest? This, Adams argued, rendered all colonists potentially "slaves of a slave of the servants of a minister of state."

A "grievous innovation," Adams labeled the creation of the admiralty courts, presided over by judges and excluding juries. This institution violated the ancient English rights guaranteed by the

Magna Carta of 1215, the right to trial by a jury of one's peers. In challenging the admiralty courts, Adams did not call upon the colonies to introduce any new concept, but merely to uphold possession of the old. It was the act of tyranny, not the colonial protest of it, that was an innovation. Nor was the tyrannical innovation limited to violation of the ancient right of jury trial. It attacked the even older principle of regulating society by laws rather than by men. Only strong and beneficial laws could protect the people against the actions of "weak or wicked" men. Human beings were subject to error, passion, whim, prejudice, self-interest, and myriad other forms of corruption, but the law was a bulwark against such harmful symptoms of impermanence.

**The Last Word:** Investing absolute authority in any one person or set of people is inherently hazardous because it consigns management to an arbitrary basis. Law—rules and policies formulated for the common good of the common enterprise—trumps the force of any one personality or will. Management must begin by managing power, which means defining its limits and providing for the enforcement of the limits it defines.

## Lesson 35
## Running a Miniature Meritocracy

*I sometimes in my sprightly moments consider myself, in my great chair at school, as some dictator at the head of a commonwealth. In this little state I can discover all the great geniuses . . . in miniature. I have several renowned generals but three feet high, and several deep projecting politicians in petticoats. I have others catching and dissecting flies, accumulating remarkable pebbles, cockle shells, &c, with as ardent curiosity as any virtuoso in the Royal Society.*

—Diary, March 15, 1765

For John Adams, one of the delights of teaching school was studying his young charges as a microcosm of society, each boy and girl exhibiting, in miniature, the traits and aptitudes of the adults they would one day be. Adams enjoyed what his "great" schoolmaster's chair afforded him: a perspective from which he might observe and judge his students, creating, in his imagination, a meritocracy in miniature—a microcosmic society in which each talent and natural inclination was clearly manifested and in which a productive place for each little person could be found, reserving the leadership positions for the most able.

Alas, Adams well understood that his classroom fantasy would never play out in the real—the larger—world. Whereas he could preside over his classroom "commonwealth" as a benign dictator, all-seeing, all-knowing, empowered to match each of his students to the task most suited to him or her, no such dictator was possible or even desirable in any commonwealth built by adults. Late in life, Adams would argue good-naturedly with his friend Thomas Jefferson over the merits of a meritocracy. Whereas Jefferson had faith that natural talent would inevitably rise to power in a free and unfettered society, Adams believed that even the freest society was fraught with accidents—especially the accidents of prominent birth or financial success—which were bound frequently to elevate the naturally mediocre above the naturally deserving. For Adams, meritocracy was born a schoolmaster's fantasy and remained such. It was, he believed, folly to hope for the inevitable ascendency in society of the naturally gifted. Far better to assume that society would, from time to time, endure leadership by the dull, the undeserving, and even the wicked. Therefore, it was necessary to erect a framework of law within which the actions of men and women, of whatever aptitudes, traits, attitudes, and motives, could be contained.

**The Last Word:** In a perfect world, the best would always lead. In a perfect world, therefore, there would be no need of law. Because the world is not perfect, no enterprise—whether nation or corporate endeavor—can afford to be without law, rules, and policy so wisely formulated that they are universally accepted and adhered to as an authority superseding that of any individual. Defining leadership in terms of a personality creates a volatile organization likely doomed either to explode or simply evaporate.

**Lesson 36**

AN EMPIRE OF LAWS

---

*[G]ood government is an empire of laws.*
— "Thoughts on Government," 1776

Good government, for Adams, was not a collection of legislators—leaders—but an "empire of laws." This left open the question of how these laws should be made, and Adams offered an answer. "In a large society, inhabiting an extensive country, it is impossible that the whole should assemble to make laws." This being the case, it is necessary to "depute power from the many to a few of the most wise and good," creating an assembly that is "in miniature an exact portrait of the people at large," an assembly that "should think, feel, reason, and . . . act like them."

Adams was determined to create a government of the people, by the people, and for the people, yet a government superior to any particular person or group of people. To achieve this, he conceived of a government of law rather than of men, yet in which the law was created by the representatives of the governed. His hope was, on the one hand, to prevent representative government from becoming mob rule, while on the other to prevent its degenerating into coerced obedience to arbitrary decree.

**The Last Word:** Management balances leadership with representation of the popular will and is guided by policy designed for the common good. Management therefore requires continual vigilance, judgment, and restraint in the exercise of power, but does not surrender authority to those it both leads and represents.

**Lesson 37**

## The Divine Science of Politics

*[T]he divine science of politics is the science of social happiness.*
—"Thoughts on Government," 1776

"For forms of government let fools contest," the English poet Alexander Pope wrote. "That which is best administered is best." Quoting this passage, John Adams disagreed with it, judging that, with it, "Pope flattered tyrants too much." For "[n]othing is more certain from the history of nations and nature of man, than that some forms of government are better fitted for being well administered than others."

It was characteristic of Adams that, in refuting Pope, he would cite history as well as human nature, the two standards by which he evaluated most matters of importance. Adams was bold in building a revolution, yet it was a boldness born not of audacious innovation, but of a keen awareness of historical precedent and the unchanging principles of humanity. Tyranny, not liberty, was the momentary aberration in the course of the conduct of government. Before setting about the remaking of government, Adams found it essential to define the purpose of government. For him, it was a straightforward matter: "the happiness of society is the end of government." This being the case, "it will follow, that the form of government which communicates ease, comfort, security, or, in one word, happiness, to the greatest number of persons, and in the greatest degree, is the best." Such a government required a "foundation [of] virtue," which is self-evidently "better calculated to promote the general happiness than any other form." The problem is that "[f]ear is the foundation of most governments," and fear is a "sordid and brutal passion." To reshape government, it would be necessary to replace fear with something that appeals to the "noblest principles and most generous affections in our nature." For Adams believed that the "foundation of every government is some principle or passion in the minds of the people," not some externally defined and supported abstraction. Because of this, a good government had to be a representative government, with a legislative assembly that was "in miniature an exact portrait of the people at large."

**The Last Word:** Successful management of any enterprise is never merely a matter of administration. It is always founded in leadership that is, in turn, shaped and guided by a clear conception of the purpose—the end—for which the organization exists. If this end is both clearly defined and truly worthwhile, it will imply the form of management necessary to achieve it. In most complex, high-stakes organizations, management cannot be simply imposed from above, but must in some measure represent the entire enterprise. To the degree that everyone feels entitled to a stake in the endeavor, performance is likely to be at a high level. A corporate endeavor is not a democracy or even a republic, but it must in some way represent the best values and aspirations of all who take a part in it.

**Lesson 38**

## REVOLUTION AS EVOLUTION

*At present, it will be safest to proceed in all established modes, to which the people have been familiarized by habit.*

—"Thoughts on Government," 1776

Adams never doubted that a just government had to be a representative government, but the difficult question to resolve was just how to create a genuinely representative government. "That it may be the interest of [the] assembly to do strict justice at all times," he wrote, "it should be an equal representation, or, in other words, equal interests among the people should have equal interests in it." Achieving this would require "great care" and various regulations "to prevent unfair, partial, and corrupt elections," yet, he cautioned, such "regulations . . . may be better made in times of greater tranquility than" in the midst of a violent revolution. For the "present, it will be safest to proceed in all established modes, to which the people have been familiarized by habit." Revolution is by definition change, yet Adams was anxious to reconcile revolutionary change with continuity. He was unafraid to integrate evolution into revolution, to make the most necessary changes—paramount among which was independence from Britain—and to let other changes follow in natural course.

**The Last Word:** Authentic leadership requires a large dose of impatience, but also a willingness to use time as an ally rather than simply regard it as a foe. Unchallenged, continuity can become complacence, but, skillfully managed, it can also facilitate change by easing others into the new order. Revolutionary management is not binary, this then that, but more often a matter of degree, careful monitoring, and continual adjustment to achieve productive change.

**Lesson 39**
## Avoiding Committee Hell

*A representative assembly . . . is unfit to exercise executive power . . . [and] is still less qualified for the judicial power.*
—"Thoughts on Government," 1776

Adams defined three major functions of government: legislative, executive, and judicial. Although he believed that representation was the soul of any truly legitimate government, he did not believe that all three government functions could be vested in the representative branch, the legislature. Although the assembly was "absolutely necessary," it was "unfit to exercise the executive power, for want of two essential properties, secrecy and dispatch." An assembly is essentially a committee, which, as any manager knows only too well, is a body that has a hard time keeping a secret and an even harder time moving quickly. Adams did not suggest eliminating the committee feature of governmental management—quite the contrary, it was "absolutely necessary"—but he did not propose to assign it work of an executive nature. Similarly, the assembly could not handle the "judicial power, because it was too numerous, too slow, and too little skilled in the laws." Interpreting the rules of society—or any complex organization—requires specialists skilled in such interpretation and both accustomed and trained to render timely judgments.

**The Last Word:** Everyone in business curses committees. Adams did not. Instead, he sought to ensure that they would not be assigned tasks for which they were ill-suited and unqualified.

**Lesson 40**

NEVER CONFUSE "NECESSARY" WITH "SUFFICIENT"

*But shall the whole power of legislation rest in one assembly?*
—"Thoughts on Government," 1776

"Absolutely necessary" John Adams called the inclusion of a representative assembly in any government. But he limited the utility of the legislature to law making, and assigned the executive and judicial functions of government to two other, separate and independent branches. He did not make the mistake of confusing "necessary" with "sufficient."

**The Last Word:** Successful management identifies and defines all necessary functions, then evaluates whether or not these are sufficient to the productive conduct of the enterprise. If they are not, then additional functions need to be added. Once the necessary and sufficient functions have been established, the next task is to create the apparatus for executing the functions. As with the functions themselves, this necessary apparatus must also be made sufficient. Until that goal has been attained, the management structure of the organization is incomplete and inadequate.

## Lesson 41
## CEREMONY

*These ceremonies may be condemned by philosophy, and ridiculed by comedy, with great reason. Yet the common sense of mankind has never adopted the rigid decrees of the former, nor ever sincerely laughed with the latter.*

—Diary, June 7, 1778

While he was negotiating the Franco-American alliance, Adams was intrigued by the spectacle of Louis XVI's court, especially its daily rituals and ceremonies. He saw through these as essentially empty and therefore irrational, yet he did not disdain them. True, hollow ceremony "may be condemned by philosophy," but the mass of humanity were not philosophers. Ceremony might be irrational, but people were never entirely rational themselves, and thus a certain degree of ritualized irrationality was a necessary means of communication and communion, drawing together any common endeavor. "Something of the kind every government and every religion has," Adams observed, "and must have."

**The Last Word:** While leaders must not dismiss ceremony, it is also the "business and duty of lawgivers and philosophers . . . to endeavor to prevent . . . [ceremonial rituals] from going too far." As in most essentials of organized human behavior, Adams advocated and sought a balance of extremes. The great principle of managing any drive, any force, any power was to pit one drive, or force, or power against another and thereby achieve a productive equilibrium.

## Lesson 42
## NECESSARY FORCE

*I have long been settled in my own opinion, that neither Philosophy, nor Religion, nor Morality, nor Wisdom, nor Interest, will ever govern nations or Parties, against their Vanity, their Pride, their Resentment or Revenge, or their Avarice or Ambition. Nothing but Force and Power and Strength can restrain them.*

—Letter to Thomas Jefferson, October 9, 1787

Repeatedly, in virtually everything he wrote or said, John Adams asserted that government is essentially the management of power, and power can be managed only by a countervailing power. The peaceful arsenal of reason, of religion, of morality is ultimately incapable of restraining the force engendered by human passions. Force, power, and strength are all that may prevail.

At first glance, this vision of management seems grim indeed; however, the implications of Adams's theory are not so much grim as they are stringent and demanding. The picture presented is of a dynamic system, an economy of powers, each pushing against the other and each being pushed in return.

**The Last Word:** Management is not the use of force to crush the force of others, but to balance it, to regulate it. After all, it is the passion of each member of the enterprise that carries the enterprise forward. Without it, there is no motivation, no invention, no business. Yet, to be useful and constructive, the force of individual passions must be regulated, collectivized, and harmonized—yoked to the organization as a whole, so that no one member is permitted to hijack the enterprise, even temporarily.

## Lesson 43
## POWER, DEMOCRACY, AND TYRANNY

*We have all along contended, that a simple government, in a single assembly, whether aristocratical or democratical, must of necessity divide into two parties, each of which will be headed by some one illustrious family, and will proceed from debate and controversy to sedition and war.*

—*A Defence of the Constitutions of the Government of*
*the United States of America*, 1789

Thomas Jefferson, among others, held that democracy was the sovereign antidote to tyranny. John Adams disagreed. A simple democracy would soon become partisan, he held, and those parties would be controlled not by ideological groups, but by prominent families, with the result that the government would soon degenerate into an arena of contenders for absolute power. Tyranny was not simply the absence of democracy, it was the presence of power unchecked, unregulated. All forces—arbitrary authority as well as democratic authority—required management, which Adams defined as a matter of balancing one power against another in order to achieve the stability of equilibrium. The apparatus required to accomplish this could not be accommodated in a simple democracy, but called for a blend of direct popular representation and appointed authority in government, plus a system of checks and balances by which the legislature was checked by an executive, whose powers were nevertheless limited by the legislature, the both of which were subject to oversight and ruling in points of law by a judiciary, which lacked both legislative and executive powers.

Thomas Jefferson never wholeheartedly embraced the Constitution, which he saw as too restrictive of democracy. John Adams regarded it as nothing less than a manual of management for democracy. Jefferson believed the great safeguard of unalienable rights was the direct investment of power in the people. Adams believed that only through the careful management of power could the people's rights be safeguarded.

*Revolutionary Wisdom*

"The fundamental Article of my political Creed is, that Despotism, or unlimited Sovereignty, or absolute Power is the same in a Majority of a popular Assembly, an Aristocratical Counsel, an Oligarchical Junto and a single Emperor. Equally arbitrary cruel bloody and in every respect diabolical."

—*Letter to Thomas Jefferson, November 13, 1815*

**The Last Word:** The spirit of American democracy probably owes more to Thomas Jefferson than it does to John Adams, but the practical conduct of American government reveals the restraining hand of Adams far more than the idealistic mind of Jefferson.

**Lesson 44**

## Power Without Balance Is Government Without Law

*A simple sovereignty in one, a few, or many, has no balance, and therefore no laws.*

—Letter to Roger Sherman, July 18, 1789

John Adams did not contend that a balance of powers made for the *best* government, he maintained that it was the only way to create a *genuine* government, a *free* government—that is, a *government of laws* rather than of men. It is easy to see that an absolute monarch or dictator, ruling by fiat and whim, does not truly govern. He coerces and compels. It is less easy to see that this can be the case even if sovereignty is distributed among more than a single person, as it was in the Directory that was the product of the French Revolution. Although many shared sovereignty, there was no check on the power of this single body, and thus the result was a collective despotism, which is the absence of genuine government because law does not exist. To be sure, a set of written laws may be on the books, but if sovereign power is not balanced by other sovereign power, there is nothing to stop the sovereign from abiding by some of the laws some of the time or none of the laws some of the time, or none of the laws—ever.

Power is essential to government. It is the substance of management. Yet power is also inimical to government and to management of any kind. The regulation of power is the business both of government and of management. The only enduringly effective way of managing power is by opposing one power with another. Among the powers that require opposition is that of individual will. For this reason, power must be vested both in individuals and in laws, with the laws ultimately taking precedence over any one individual or collection of individuals within a single branch of government.

**The Last Word:** It is popular among many recent writers on management to denigrate such concepts as "company policy" in favor of individual initiative, innovation, improvisation, and even common sense. Yet these commodities are no less arbitrary than a set of written corporate policies. The Holy Grail of management is neither unchanging stability nor an indiscriminate embrace of change, but, rather, the creation of stability within change. "Company policy," mindlessly administered, can become a straitjacket, but simply discarding such policy is insanity itself.

**Lesson 45**

## Variations on a Theme

*[A]varice and ambition, vanity and pride, jealousy and envy, hatred and revenge, as well as the love of knowledge and desire of fame, are very often nothing more than various modifications of that desire for attention, consideration, and congratulations of our fellow men, which is the great spring of social activity.*

—*Discourses on Davila*, 1790–1791

So strongly did John Adams believe in the driving force of the desire for attention that, upon reflection, he concluded that much of the range of human activity could be traced to it. The importance of this insight lies in the realization that the "great spring of social activity" is in itself neither good nor evil, but the phenomena to which it gives rise may be. That is, passions as diverse as hatred and the love of knowledge both flow from the same source, a desire for attention. They are simply different "modifications" of the desire.

**The Last Word:** The lesson for leaders is to make no attempt to excite or to stem the desire for attention. It is, after all, a force of nature and cannot be altered. Instead, leadership efforts must be focused on the "modifications," on nurturing and shaping the forms taken by the underlying drive.

**Lesson 46**

## THE TROUBLE WITH HEROES

*Heroes, proceed! What bounds your pride shall hold?*
*What check restrain your thirst of power and gold?*
—Samuel Johnson, quoted by Adams in *Discourses on Davila,* 1790–1791

The answer to the questions posed by Johnson, Adams wrote, "can be none other than this, that, as nature has established in the bosoms of heroes no limits to those passions; and as the world, instead of restraining, encourages them, the check must be in the form of government."

No enterprise, whether nation or corporate endeavor, can be carried exclusively on the backs of heroes—though every organization requires at least a few. Every manager knows the value of what old-timers used to call "spark plugs" or "ramrods," the individuals who light fires under others, who bring order out of chaos, who get things done. They're indispensible. The danger, however, is that these heroes begin to hijack the entire enterprise. They become what Adams would have called the "aristocrats" of the enterprise, the people who assume inordinate amounts of authority and influence, ultimately pulling the organization into a form of arbitrary leadership that is without check. Government, Adams believed, existed not to suppress, let alone eliminate heroes, but to check and regulate their actions, if necessary by pitting one set of heroes against another in a system that balanced power against power for the purpose of producing controllable and therefore useful power.

*Revolutionary Wisdom*

"No man was ever contented with any given share of his human adoration. When Caesar declared that he had lived enough in glory, Caesar might deceive himself, but he did not deceive the world, who saw his declaration contradicted by every action of his subsequent life. Man constantly craves for more, even when he has no rival."

—*Discourses on Davila, 1790–1791*

**The Last Word:** Value and celebrate the heroes of your organization, but never subordinate the enterprise to them. A cult of personality can achieve short-term goals, but it is inimical to the endurance of any collective endeavor.

## Lesson 47
## On the Necessity of Management

*If all decorum, discipline, and subordination are to be destroyed, and universal Pyrrhonism, anarchy, and insecurity of property are to be introduced, nations will soon wish their books in ashes, seek for darkness and ignorance, superstition and fanaticism, as blessings, and follow the standard of the first mad despot, who . . . will endeavor to obtain them.*
— *Discourses on Davila*, 1790–1791

For Adams, the "triumph" of the French Revolution was an example of "Pyrrhonism," a Pyrrhic victory, a win at ruinous cost.

What, precisely, was the cost of defeating "all decorum, discipline, and subordination"? Ultimately, the rebirth of the dark ages, the ages of feudal anarchy and absolute submission to "the first mad despot" who promises a reign of "darkness and ignorance, superstition and fanaticism."

The great irony of authority is that it continually tempts its own destruction, but, if destroyed, it creates the climate in which it is quickly reestablished—typically on the most arbitrary, violent, and destructive of terms. Anarchy is the vacuum into which dictatorship rushes. But not only is dictatorship no viable alternative to anarchy, it is itself a form of anarchy: arbitrary authority sustainable only by unnatural force. The only genuine, durable, and workable alternative to chaos and dictatorship is a government that incorporates "decorum, discipline, and subordination"—in short, that manages power—for the benefit of collective enterprise rather than for one or a few or even, apparently, of the masses.

In contrast to Jefferson and his followers, Adams did not believe in "pure" democracy, the direct investment of all authority in the people. The degree to which power may be shared among the many versus the few is open to continual debate and adjustment in American government. In a business endeavor, however, the fate of "pure" democracy is even less certain if only because the utility of such a management scheme is highly questionable.

**The Last Word:** Every manager must decide how to manage power, positioning that management somewhere between the extremes of relinquishing all decision making to the group or acting at all times unilaterally. There is no easy answer, but there must be an answer, since the management of power is the issue on which all other aspects of management depend. Failure to answer the question means drift. Looking for an anchor? Whatever else you assume, assume the absolute necessity of management. Then set about answering the question in practical detail.

## Lesson 48
## THE STUBBORN ARISTOCRATS

*[Aristocrats] are the most difficult Animals to manage. . . . They will not suffer themselves to be governed.*

—Letter to Thomas Jefferson, July 9, 1813

For Adams, an "aristocrat" was anyone who made it his business to commandeer the influence of others, to command (in a representative democracy) at least two votes, his own and someone else's. In practice, aristocrats wield disproportionate influence in a society. The source of their aristocracy might be inherited—noble birth— but it might also be natural talent, intellect, beauty, charisma, or it might be wealth and property.

The influence any particular aristocrat or group of aristocrats (an aristocracy) exercises might be beneficial to society. Certainly, that was Thomas Jefferson's hope and belief: that a free government would make room for the rise of a natural aristocracy—a meritocracy—ruled by the best and the brightest. Adams conceded that this was possible, but he pointed out that it would not occur inevitably or automatically and that, really, there was no effective way to ensure the rise of a natural aristocracy. It was just as likely that some other form of aristocracy would seize undue influence, to the detriment, even the ruin, of government and society.

It was not enough, therefore, merely to hope for a "good" or "worthy" aristocracy. Whatever form it took, beneficial or harmful, Adams argued, aristocracy was inherently destructive to free government because aristocrats refuse to be governed and, what is more, "not only exert all their own Subtilty, Industry and courage, but they employ the Commonalty, to knock to pieces every Plan and Model that the most honest Architects in Legislation can invent to keep them within bounds." Thus, for example, the medieval peasant may be willing to die in defense of the very lord who oppresses him, or, these days, the retail clerk in a rural megastore may vote not for the presidential candidate who promises him government-subsidized health care and a higher minimum wage, but the one who advocates lower taxes for the very wealthy. Crazy? Not according to Adams, who saw a basic human drive to submit to and support an aristocracy. And that was a real danger to free government.

**The Last Word:** In your business, your organization, your department, you want a coterie of aristocrats—the best, the brightest, the most innovative, the most productive—yet you must also be wary of them, wary of their tendency to usurp power and to go it alone, to refuse to be team players, and to preempt influence that should be yours and yours alone. Management must nurture and maintain a vital "aristocracy" even while controlling and curbing its influence. A contradiction? A paradox? Nobody said management was easy.

**Lesson 49**

Information Management

*The causes that impede political knowledge would fill a hundred volumes.*

—Letter to John Taylor, April 15, 1814

No republic could long endure, Adams believed, as a government of ignorant people. The more knowledge the more people have—especially "political knowledge"—the greater the chances that a free republican government will endure and prosper. Toward this end, he believed that a government should spare no expense to educate the people as far as they may be educated; inevitably, some would merit more education than others.

All of this notwithstanding, in 1798, Adams signed into law the notorious and controversial Alien and Sedition Acts. The sedition legislation in particular included what were, effectively, provisions to abridge both the rights of assembly and of free speech:

> SECTION 1. Be it enacted by the Senate and House of Representatives of the United States of America, in Congress assembled, That if any persons shall unlawfully combine or conspire together, with intent to oppose any measure or measures of the government of the United States . . . , they shall be deemed guilty of a high misdemeanor . . .

> SEC. 2. And be it further enacted, That if any person shall write, print, utter or publish, or shall cause or procure to be written, printed, uttered or published, or shall knowingly and willingly assist or aid in writing, printing, uttering or publishing any false, scandalous and malicious writing or

writings against the government of the United States, or either house of the Congress of the United States, or the President of the United States, with intent to defame the said government, or either house of the said Congress, or the said President, or to bring them, or either of them, into contempt or disrepute; or to excite against them, or either or any of them, the hatred of the good people of the United States . . . then such person . . . shall be punished by a fine not exceeding two thousand dollars, and by imprisonment not exceeding two years.

Admirers of and apologists for John Adams have always stumbled over the Alien and Sedition Acts, which, no matter how one looks at them, smack unmistakably of tyranny. We need not debate the wisdom of these acts here. Suffice it to say that Adams feared that the fruits of the American Revolution—a struggling young republic—were in danger of being plucked by the bloody hands of those intoxicated by the much more radical French Revolution, and he favored giving Congress tools by which expression of the most radical ideas might be curbed in America.

*Revolutionary Wisdom*

"Aristotle wrote the History and description of Eighteen hundred Republicks, which existed before his time. Cicero wrote two Volumes of discourses on Government, which, perhaps, were worth all the rest of his Works. The Works of Livy and Tacitus etc that are lost, would be more interesting than all that remain. Fifty Gospells have been destroyed, and where are St. Lukes World of Books that had been written? If you ask my Opinion, who has committed all the havoc? I will answer you candidly. Ecclesiastical and Imperial Despotism has done it, to conceal their Frauds.

—*Letter to Thomas Jefferson, July 9, 1813*

**The Last Word:** For leaders of any enterprise today, the lesson is this: The management of information is often necessary for the good of the organization. Positive public relations is important. Secrets must sometimes be kept. Morale needs to be nurtured. Problems can be made to seem either ruinous or challenging or rich in opportunity, depending how information concerning them is handled, crafted, and finally presented—or withheld. These are facts, and they cannot be ignored. But when does information management become censorship? When does interpretation become distortion? When is "spin" simply a lie, and secrecy destructive? These are questions—restless, insistent, urgent, vital—and they must be answered, both in general principle and in specific application, case after case.

**Lesson 50**

ONE CONSEQUENCE OF EDUCATION

*The more you educate, without a balance in government, the more aristocratical will the people and the government be.*

—Letter to John Taylor, April 15, 1814

John Adams so valued education that he believed it was one of the very few commodities on which governments should spare no expense. Yet, for him, even education, good as it was, was not an *absolute* good. In a government that failed to observe the cardinal principle of balance of powers—the establishment of a system that creates equilibrium by using power to oppose power—education naturally produces aristocracy. Take Adams's alma mater, Harvard University. "Say that, in almost two hundred years, there have been three or four thousand educated from perhaps two or three millions of people. Are not these aristocrats? or, in other words, have they not had more influence than any equal number of uneducated men?" The point is not that education is good or bad, but that, like any other ingredient, commodity, attitude, idea, authority, force, or other element in an organization, it cannot be considered in a vacuum.

**The Last Word:** Government, like any other form of management, relates element to element, always in the context of the enterprise and never in isolation. For the manager, there is no absolute good or bad. Everything is evaluated and used in relation to everything else in the system.

## Lesson 51
## "INEQUALITIES ARE A PART OF THE NATURAL HISTORY OF MAN"

*That all men are born to equal rights is true. . . . But to teach that all men are born with equal powers and faculties, to equal influence in society, to equal property and advantages through life, is as gross a fraud, as glaring an imposition on the credulity of the people, as ever was practiced by monks, by Druids, by Brahmins, by priests of the immortal Lama, or by the self-styled philosophers of the French revolution.*

—Letter to John Taylor, April 17–18, 1814

The important thing about recognizing the equality of human rights yet the inequality of all other human attributes is that, while government must uphold universal justice under the law—equality of rights—it must also accommodate the results of inequality, the reality that some people, by virtue of their property, their wealth, their abilities, their eloquence, their charisma, or even their birth, will be more influential in society that others. No genuinely free—non-coercive—government can ignore this basic reality. The bus driver has, under the law, rights equal to those of the wealthy industrialist, yet it is also true that the wealthy industrialist will have more influence on society than the bus driver.

*Revolutionary Wisdom*
"Now to what higher object, to what greater character, can any mortal aspire than to be possessed of all this knowledge, well digested and ready at command, to assist the feeble and friendless, to discountenance the haughty and lawless, to procure redress of wrongs, the advancement of right, to assert

and maintain liberty and virtue, to discourage and abolish tyranny and vice."

—*Letter to Jonathan Sewall, October 1759*

**The Last Word:** As a leader, you must manage your organization to take maximum advantage of people who have the greatest abilities in particular fields. If you run an advertising agency, you cannot afford to give everyone an equal shot at running the art department, or heading up sales, or being chief copywriter. People have unequal talent and experience. Still, you must treat everyone as valuable, deserving of respect and uniformly fair treatment. Adams's message was that inequality was real, and dealing with it required nothing much more than common sense. Yet the well-meaning ideologues of the American Revolution and the years that immediately followed were reluctant and did not want to hear such a message. Their reluctance did not discourage Adams. It was, after all, a most important message.

# CHAPTER 4

# Power

## Lesson 52
## OF LAWLESS BULLS

*[T]hey are lawless bulls; they roar and bluster, defy all control, and some-*
*times murder their proper owner.*

—Diary, June 14, 1756

For Adams, "passion" was essential to any great enterprise, and yet, he wrote, he "is not a wise man, and is unfit to fill any important station in society, that has left one passion in his soul unsubdued." As necessary as passion was, it was yet more necessary to "subdue"—control, regulate, and direct—passion. A "love of glory" is an indispensible passion in a military leader; nevertheless, "love of glory will make a General sacrifice the interest of his nation to his own fame." Other passions, including avarice, envy, and even love, have proven destructive to society, yet also essential to its advance. Adams knew better than to advocate the extinguishment of passion—that was undesirable and, in any case, impossible—but he stressed the absolute necessity of binding passions "fast" and bringing them "under the yoke." The passions, "untamed . . . are lawless bulls," but "properly inured to obedience, they take their places under the yoke without noise, and labor vigorously in their master's service."

The trouble with the majority of history's "great men," Adams believed, was their passion for power, its acquisition and its use. Their belief was that power was the key to leading others. Adams, in contrast, believed that controlling power was the key, bringing the raging bull under the "yoke," properly inuring him to obedience, and thereby transforming his brute force into useful labor.

*Revolutionary Wisdom*
"There is danger from all men. The only maxim of a free government ought to be to trust no man living with power to endanger the public liberty."
—*"Notes for an Oration at Braintree, Massachusetts,"* 1772

**The Last Word:** Mistaking mere power for leadership is not only unproductive, but both generally destructive and specifically self-destructive. Leadership is the management of power—not the diminishment or suppression of it, but the taming of it in accordance with principles and objectives formulated with the collective, ongoing good of the enterprise in mind.

## Lesson 53
## Ajax and Ulysses

*[A] man of sense would hold even the true martial qualities, courage, strength, and skill in war, in a much lower estimation than the attributes of wisdom and virtue.*

—"On Private Revenge, No. III," *Boston Gazette*, September 5, 1763

Adams was a lover of the classics in Latin and Greek. He reminded the readers of his early essay "On Private Revenge, No. III" that the "competition between Ajax and Ulysses is well known" and went on to quote a passage from the Roman poet Ovid's *Metamorphoses*: "You show strength without thought," says Ovid's Ulysses to Ajax. "I am mindful of the future. You are able to fight; you display only the body, I the spirit. Minds are stronger than hands—all force is in them." It was this belief, ultimately, that gave Adams the courage to hope and even to believe that a revolution against England, the most formidable military power on earth, would succeed. Adams believed the American position was born of superior intellect, whereas the English hold on its colony was the product of indefensible reasoning. American had right on its side. The Crown and Parliament, on the other hand, were wrong. Although they possessed the advantage in force, theirs was "strength without thought."

**The Last Word:** Draw strength from a great idea. Never doubt the power of a plan.

**Lesson 54**

## THE DESIRE OF DOMINION

*The desire of dominion, that great principle by which we have attempted
to account for so much good and so much evil, is, when properly restrained,
a very useful and noble movement of the human mind.*

—*A Dissertation on the Canon and Feudal Law*, 1765

Adams defined *dominion* as the desire for sovereignty or control of
a place or people and saw it as a powerful force in the affairs of
the world. Like any other force, it was, in itself, neither good nor
evil, yet responsible for both good and evil. If "properly restrained,"
dominion could be "a very useful and noble movement of the human
mind," nothing less than a driver of civilization. "But when such
restraints are taken off, it becomes an encroaching, grasping, restless, and ungovernable power," spawning "numberless . . . systems of
iniquity contrived by the great for the gratification of this passion
in themselves." In this particular essay, the 1765 *Dissertation on the
Canon and Feudal Law*, the system of iniquity Adams focused on
was the canon law (which gave the Church arbitrary and untram-
meled power) and the feudal law (which gave lords and nobles similar
authority). But the principle—that any number of forces operating
in the world were natural and necessary, but were useful rather than
destructive only when properly restrained—informed all of Adams's
thought lifelong.

*Revolutionary Wisdom*
"Metaphysicians and politicians may dispute forever, but they will never find any other moral principle or foundation of rule or obedience, than the consent of governors and governed."
—*Novanglus*, 1774–1775

**The Last Word:** Too many leaders see power as a good in itself, an end rather than a means. But sound management is the management of power, the transformation of this morally and creatively neutral commodity—capable of either building or destruction, of good or ill—into a means of achieving the positive goals of the enterprise. Sound management sees power as a tool and a means, never an end in itself.

**Lesson 55**

## LET NO ONE BUT *YOU* DEFINE WHAT *YOU* DO

*We are not exciting a rebellion.*

—*Novanglus,* 1774–1775

To the Loyalist assertion that "[i]t is a universal truth, that he that would excite a rebellion, is at heart as great a tyrant as ever wielded the iron rod of oppression," John Adams responded: "Be it so. We are not exciting a rebellion. Opposition, nay, open, avowed resistance by arms, against usurpation and lawless violence, is not rebellion by the law of God or the land. Resistance to lawful authority makes rebellion," but resistance to tyranny is a defense of rights.

**The Last Word:** General George S. Patton Jr. held as a prime tenet of strategy that the enemy should never be allowed to choose the field of battle. Similarly, it is fatal to allow others to define *your* intentions, *your* aims, *your* objectives. Any such attempts must be met aggressively and corrected. Know what you are about, and make it your business to project this definition throughout your organization. Be vigilant. Control the terms on which you propose to act and on which you act in actuality. Let no one hijack your intentions.

## Lesson 56
## MANAGING THE "SOCIAL AFFECTION"

---

*There is, in the human Breast, a social Affection.*
—Letter to Abigail Adams, October 29, 1775

In a letter to his wife written early in the Revolution, Adams expressed his belief that human beings were governed by what he called a "social affection." Although this quality, impulse, instinct, or drive "extends to our whole Species," it does so "faintly indeed." The "Nation, Kingdom, or Community to which We belong is embraced by it more vigorously," however, and "it is stronger still towards the Province to which we belong, and in which We had our birth." The social affection is even more intense "as We descend to the County, Town, Parish, Neighbourhood, and Family, which We call our own." And therein lay the problem for creating a nation; for the social affection is "often so powerful as to become partial" on these local levels, sufficiently powerful "to blind our Eyes, to darken our Understandings and pervert our Wills." For Adams, this was no abstraction, for he admitted suffering from "this Infirmity," which manifested itself in "overweening Prejudice in favour of New England." Acknowledging this, he knew it must be overcome, so that the social affection could be attached directly to the entire nation. Persuading each citizen to do likewise was the essence of creating a national union as opposed to a collection of separate colonies populated by self-interested individual men and women.

*Revolutionary Wisdom*

"I forgot to remark your Preference to Savage over civilized life. I have Something to say upon that Subject. If I am in Error, you can set me Right, but by all I know of one or the other I would rather be the poorest Man in France or England, with sound health of Body and Mind, than the proudest King, Sachem or Warriour of any Tribe of Savages in America."

—*Letter to Thomas Jefferson, February 3, 1812*

**The Last Word:** Creating throughout an organization a deep identification with the enterprise is always an urgent imperative of management. It requires an understanding of the "social affection," including both a willingness to acknowledge it and to see beyond it or, rather, to extend it beyond the local to the outer limits of the common good.

## Lesson 57
### BAD MANAGEMENT AS A REASON FOR REVOLUTION

*[B]y an act of Parliament, we are put out of the royal protection, and consequently discharged from our allegiance.*

—"Thoughts on Government," 1776

Dedicated to the law, attorney John Adams argued during the years leading up to the American Revolution that there was no legal basis for Parliamentary sovereignty over the American colonies because the colonies were not—and could not, in practical terms, ever be—represented in Parliament. Turning to the original charters of the colonies, he did affirm the legality of an ongoing allegiance to the king, since it was the king who had granted the charters; however, in permitting Parliament to tax the colonies and to pass other laws restricting and later punishing the colonies, Adams argued, the king "put [us] out of the royal protection," which meant that the king effectively "discharged [us] from our allegiance" to him.

As John Adams conceived it, the American Revolution was not only morally justified, it was an entirely legal—contractual—action. Parliament never had legal sovereignty over the colonies, which, however, owed allegiance to the king—*so long as the king extended his protection over the colonies*. When the king abrogated that protection by illegally consigning administration of the colonies to Parliament, he also abrogated the contract that had existed between himself and the colonies. In effect, the American Revolution was the product of King George III's bad management. He misunderstood the nature of the connection between the colonies and Britain, and, in his attempt to assert tighter control over the colonies by means of Parliament, he introduced a deal breaker.

*Revolutionary Wisdom*

"Your letter of Aug. 15 [1823] was received in due time, and with the welcome of every thing which comes from you. With its opinions on the difficulties of revolutions, from despotism to freedom, I very much concur. The generation which commences a revolution can rarely compleat it. Habituated from their infancy to passive submission of body and mind to their kings and priests, they are not qualified, when called on, to think and provide for themselves and their inexperience, their ignorance and bigotry make them instruments often, in the hands of the Bonapartes and Iturbides to defeat their own rights and purposes."

—*Thomas Jefferson, letter to John Adams, September 4, 1823*

**The Last Word:** Failing to understand the legal as well as moral and ethical nature of the relationships that apply in any high-stakes enterprise can be fatal. Assertion of right and exercise of force alone are the worst of bad management and can neither preserve nor perpetuate illegal, illegitimate, or otherwise dysfunctional relationships.

## Lesson 58
## CHECKS AND BALANCES

*And all these errors ought to be corrected and defects supplied by some controlling power.*

—"Thoughts on Government," 1776

Adams championed representation through a bicameral legislature—much like the modern Congress, consisting of an upper and lower house, one apportioned by state, the other in proportion to population—as well as a government of three major, independent branches, legislative, executive, and judicial. His rationale for both of these features of government was to prevent any one group from assuming absolute control. "A single assembly," he wrote, "is liable to all the vices, follies, and frailties of an individual." In effect, it might function as a kind of collective person, "subject to fits of humor, starts of passion, flights of enthusiasm, partialities, or prejudice, and consequently productive of hasty results and absurd judgments." It was these "errors" and "defects" that required correction by "some controlling power."

But what power would control the controlling power?

Adams conceived government as the management of power, and he regarded power both as a commodity requiring management and as one capable of applying management. Power was to be managed by countervailing power. Thus, the "lower," popularly elected assembly was to be checked and balanced by an "upper" assembly, whose members would be appointed by an executive. Even this balanced, bicameral legislature was to be checked and balanced by an executive (whose powers were simultaneously limited by the legislature) and by an independent judiciary (which checked and balanced both the legislature and the executive, but which lacked legislative and executive powers of its own).

*Revolutionary Wisdom*

"The foundation of every government is some principle or passion in the minds of the people. The noblest principles and most generous affections in our nature, then, have the fairest chance to support the noblest and most generous models of government."

—*"Thoughts on Government,"* 1776

**The Last Word:** Perhaps the single greatest contribution Adams made to American government was the principle that good government—sound management—required both an apparatus for taking action as well as an equally powerful apparatus for restraining action.

**Lesson 59**

ON REVOLUTION

*The Furnace of Affliction produces Refinement, in States as well as Individuals.*

—John Adams, letter to Abigail Adams, July 3, 1776

On the eve of the declaration of independence, Adams wrote to his wife to explain his conception of violent revolution. It was, he said, the equivalent of a refining furnace, combining an ordeal, a process, and a demand. Revolution was a process of purification and also demanded a "Purification from our Vices" as well as "an Augmentation of our Virtues." Specifically, Adams pointed out that revolution would give the "People . . . unbounded Power." For a Samuel Adams or a Thomas Jefferson, this was a consummation devoutly to be wished. For the management-minded Adams, however, it was a necessary effect and phase of revolution, but it could not be permitted to stand. The "People," Adams wrote, "are extreamly addicted to Corruption and Venality." In this, they are no different from "the Great." Too many advocates of revolution, Adams believed, had an unthinking faith in "the people," believing them to be naturally virtuous (much as they considered the "great" and the powerful to be naturally corrupt). Adams did not contend that "the people" were inferior to members of what hitherto had been the ruling class. He did not denigrate the common as compared with "the Great." But neither did he believe that the quality of commonness conferred any special virtue. Common or great, people are people, subject to the same vices if their power remains unbounded.

*Revolutionary Wisdom*

"Yesterday, the greatest question was decided which ever was debated in America, and a greater perhaps never was nor will be decided among men. A resolution was passed without one dissenting colony, 'that these United Colonies are, and of right ought to be, free and independent States.'"

—*Letter to Abigail Adams, July 3, 1776*

**The Last Word:** As excited as John Adams was by the accomplished fact of a declaration of independence and the revolution under way to secure that independence in fact, he confessed to Abigail that he was "not without Apprehensions" as a result of the people having acquired, of a sudden, so much power. He well knew that the management of this new authority would become the business of sustaining the revolution to a successful end.

## Lesson 60
## Character

*I answered, with utmost frankness, that I thought him a perfectly honest man, with an amiable and excellent heart, and the most important character at that time among us; for he was the centre of the Union.*
—Manuscript autobiography, portion covering 1778,
regarding George Washington

Shortly after the Continental Congress commissioned John Adams to sail to Europe as an emissary of the emerging republic, General Henry Knox had dinner with him in Braintree, Massachusetts. He asked Adams his opinion of George Washington, the man Adams himself had nominated as commander in chief of the Continental Army. Adams replied that he thought Washington a "perfectly honest man" and the "most important character . . . among us," because he was the "centre of the Union." Adams recognized in Washington military experience and ability, courage, and skill; but he also understood that the *character* of the man made him a symbol of the revolutionary endeavor, a figure around which the Union could rally and, indeed, crystallize.

Knox observed that Washington's character was also of utmost importance in Europe and needed, therefore, to be "supported" by the emissary of the Continental Congress. "I replied," Adams wrote, that "he might depend upon it, that, both from principle and affection, public and private, I should do my utmost to support his character, at all times and in all places."

John Adams was wary of political movements built around personalities. He was, in fact, unshakeable in his conviction that no government could be sustained by a personality, no matter how noble, and that the rule of law had always to take precedence over the rule of men. Yet he did not dismiss the importance of great and good men and women in a republic. Fully recognizing and appreciating the symbolic import with which his countrymen had invested George Washington, Adams was determined to make the most of it. Deeply convinced of the quality of Washington's character—publicly and personally—Adams set about conveying it to the nations of Europe as an aid to winning their recognition and even their alliance.

**The Last Word:** In the good character of a leader people perceive the nature, values, and prospects of the enterprise he leads.

## Lesson 61
## GREAT POWER GROWS GREATER

*Power naturally grows. Why? Because human passions are insatiable. But that power alone can grow which already is too great; that which is unchecked; that which has no equal power to control it.*
— Letter to Roger Sherman, July 18, 1789

Most of John Adams's revolutionary colleagues believed that good government was easily within the human capacity to create. Think hard enough, reason long enough, and the best system would emerge. Adams, however, was remarkably modern in his belief that much about the nature of government was, at least potentially, beyond the human capacity to control. Much as Sigmund Freud would write a century and more later, Adams believed the human passions insatiable, essentially ungovernable, except when opposed—and balanced—by other passions. The product of passions was, as Adams saw it, a hunger for power. Because the passions were insatiable, the hunger for power was potentially unappeasable. The result? "Power naturally grows."

Stopping here, the situation seems hopeless, at least as far as the prospects for free government go. But Adams did not stop here. While the growth of power is a natural phenomenon and therefore is inevitable as any other aspect of reality, the only power that actually grows, Adams argued, is power that is already too great—power unchecked by an "equal power to control it." Allow no unchecked power to exist in government, and nature can be controlled—managed.

*Revolutionary Wisdom*

"In our constitution the sovereignty,—that is, the legislative power,—is divided into three branches. The house and senate are equal, but the third branch, though essential, is not equal. The president must pass judgment upon every law; but in some cases his judgment may be overruled. These cases will be such as attack his constitutional power; it is, therefore, certain he has not equal power to defend himself, or the constitution, or the judicial power, as the senate and house have."

—*Letter to Roger Sherman, July 18, 1789*

**The Last Word:** As the painter's material is paint, so the leader's material is power. As the painter controls her material, balancing one color against another, composing one shape in opposition to another, so a leader controls power, always balancing, opposing, juxtaposing, and harmonizing. This is the management of power.

**Lesson 62**
## Reason and Passion

*Reason holds the helm, but passions are the gales.*
—*Discourses on Davila*, 1790–1791

John Adams lived in an era often called the Age of Reason. Among most people of a philosophical turn of mind, rationality—reason, cognition, the conscious mind—was held to be of greater value than the so-called "passions," which were seen as low, primitive, difficult to govern, and essentially destructive. No man venerated reason more than John Adams. He believed that the government of a free republic had to be designed with the greatest degree of rationality. He believed that the prime object of government was to rationalize power, which in governments dominated by a hereditary aristocracy on the one hand or a democratic mob on the other, was arbitrary, whimsical, and essentially irrational. Yet Adams neither rejected nor denigrated the passions. For him these were facts—and you cannot reject or denigrate facts—but, even more important, they were necessary to achieving anything of value in a society. Reason was about regulation and control, but, without passions, there was nothing—no force—to control, no energy to harness for the purpose of building a civilization. No one would deny that a helm is crucial to a sailing ship, but without the "gales" to drive it, there is no course to steer.

**The Last Word:** Do not elevate the means of control over the forces that give those means a reason for being. Effective leadership tends the helm but never forgets the gale that propels the ship.

## Lesson 63
### MANAGING INFLUENCE

*Please to remember that birth confers no right on one more than another! But birth naturally and unavoidably produces more influence in society, in some more than in others; and the superiority of influence is aristocracy.*

—Letter to John Taylor, April 15, 1814

Supporters of democracy often define this form of government as one in which birth—noble lineage, for example—plays no role. Adams strongly disagreed. He insisted that, in a free government, birth conferred no special rights under law. Under law, all people were perfectly equal. Nevertheless, the fact of birth makes some people more influential in society than others, and, moreover, it does so "naturally and unavoidably," regardless of what form of government is in force. To the degree that a certain set of people have more influence than others, that set constitutes an aristocracy—again, without regard to the form of government officially instituted. This was neither an inherently bad nor good thing, Adams believed. It was simply reality, and because it was reality, it had to be addressed.

Getting ahead in business, cynics have long grumbled, is as much a matter of "who you know" as it is of "what you know." The anticipated response to this statement is a knowing shake of the head as an acknowledgment of the universal injustice of the "real world." But wouldn't it be far more productive not to shake your head, but instead to acknowledge that influence is important in any business and that, therefore, you should make it your business to acquire influence?

*Revolutionary Wisdom*

"If you allow there are natural inequalities of abilities, consider the effects that the genius of Alexander produced! They are visible to this day. And what effect has the genius of Napoleon produced? They will be felt for three thousand years to come. What effect have the genius of Washington and Franklin produced? Had these men no more influence in society than the ordinary average of other men? Genius is sometimes long lived; and it has accumulated fame, wealth, and power, greater than can be commanded by millions of ordinary citizens. These advantages are sometimes applied to good purposes, and sometimes to bad."

—*Letter to John Taylor, April 15, 1814*

**The Last Word:** Instead of proudly hunkering down with "what you know," the more productive course is to identify the people in your industry, field, company, and department who clearly wield the most influence and then get to know them and get them to know you. "What you know" and "who you know" are not mutually exclusive commodities. Quite the contrary, they offer the opportunities of synergy. Combine skill, knowledge, brains, and experience with a connection to the movers and shakers around you, and you have transformed yourself into a formidable competitor.

CHAPTER 5

# Duty

## Lesson 64
### EMBRACE THE DRUDGERY OF STEWARDSHIP

*Very often shepherds that are hired to take care of their masters' sheep go about their own concerns and leave the flock to the care of their dog. So bishops, who are appointed to oversee the flock of Christ, take the fees themselves but leave the drudgery to their dogs, that is, curates and understrappers.*

—Diary, February 15, 1756

The great weakness and evil of humanity, Adams believed, was a lust for power. Like any other potentially destructive force—fire, for instance—that drive could be harnessed for the general good. It could be managed, and it was to the management of power that Adams dedicated his life and political career.

Among the many management techniques he advocated, paramount was the leader's embrace of the full spectrum of stewardship. The leader who emulated the bad shepherd, who delegated the drudgery of herding to his dogs, or who modeled himself on the corrupt bishop, who left his flock in the hands of "understrappers," was no true leader at all, but merely a human being who had surrendered to human weakness: a hunger for the trappings, the emoluments—

the perks—of power coupled to a revulsion from the responsibilities that power entails.

**The Last Word:** True leadership is stewardship. The great leaders are the great servants.

## Lesson 65

### See Beyond Both Reason and Mystification

*[T]he design of Christianity was not to make men good riddle-solvers, or good mystery-mongers, but good men, good magistrates, and good subjects, good husbands and good wives, good parents and good children, good masters and good servants.*

—Diary, February 18, 1756

John Adams lived in what has been called the Age of Reason, and, indeed, it was an appeal to rationality—to reason—that provided the bedrock of the American Revolution. Adams and others took pains to demonstrate that a government in which power was hereditary was irrational, unreasonable, and therefore contrary to both nature and human nature. Yet Adams was ever wary of clinging to any one thing too tightly. As he saw it, neither passion nor reason was in itself sufficient to guide the management of any great enterprise, least of all a nation.

Adams grew up in the Congregational Church, inheritor of the Puritan traditions of New England's founders. He was a religious man, yet he distrusted what he saw as the extremes of religiosity—irrational, emotional transport on the one hand, and mere intellectualism, the unfeeling embrace of rationality, on the other. In the hands of many preachers and religious thinkers, Christianity had become an intellectual exercise, the solving of riddles. For others, it was a thing entirely beyond rationality, a matter of dark mystery. Both of these extremes, Adams believed, missed the essence of Christianity, which was the improvement of humanity. For Adams, beliefs, creeds, morals, governments, and systems of religion were never merely aids or motives to reason on the one hand or passion on the other. They were aids and motives to useful action and righteous behavior.

*Revolutionary Wisdom*

"The question before the human race is, Whether the God of nature shall govern the World by his own laws, or Whether Priests and Kings shall rule it by fictitious Miracles? or, in other Words, whether Authority is originally in the People? or whether it has descended for 1800 Years in a succession of Popes and Bishops, or brought down from Heaven by the holy Ghost in the form of a Dove, in a Phyal of holy Oil?"

—*Letter to Thomas Jefferson, June 20, 1815*

**The Last Word:** Management, whether of an enterprise or simply of oneself, requires principles, but cannot rest on them. Management is complete only when it puts principles into the service of productive acts and ethical conduct.

**Lesson 66**
BEWARE THE LOVE OF FAME

*The love of fame naturally betrays a man into several weaknesses and fopperies that tend very much to diminish his reputation, and so defeat itself.*

—Diary, May 3, 1756

A wariness of the hunger for fame was hardly original with John Adams or unique to him. In the eighteenth century, it was a commonplace cautionary sentiment, as it is today. The difference in Adams's case was his self-awareness: "Vanity," he wrote in his diary, "I am sensible, is my cardinal vice and cardinal folly." He thought himself in "continual danger" of pursuing empty fame and believed that only the "strictest caution and watchfulness" over himself could control this tendency.

**The Last Word:** "Know thyself," the Delphic Oracle of ancient Greece proclaimed. Adams knew himself, warts and all. When he made moral and ethical generalizations, they sprang from intimate self-awareness rather than book-learned abstraction. For this reason, they were powerful precepts of leadership and they helped to define—for him and others—the duties of a leader.

**Lesson 67**

## UNION IS ALL

---

*. . . were it not for the capacity of uniting with others . . .*
—"On Private Revenge," *Boston Gazette*, August 1, 1763

In his earliest published writing, John Adams pondered the status of humankind within the animal kingdom. Human beings, he argued, enjoyed "but little elevation above the bear or the tiger"; indeed, people would hold "an inferior rank in the scale of being, and would have a worse prospect of happiness than those creatures, were it not for the capacity of uniting with others." As a person "comes originally from the hands of his Creator," he does not possess this capacity, but is motivated only by "self-love or self-preservation." Would such a primal existence be "worth preserving?" Adams asked. "In this savage state, courage, hardiness, activity, and strength, the virtues of the other brutes, are the only excellencies to which man can aspire." Any perceived injury or insult would be settled in a brutish manner, with each man "his own avenger." In any dispute, the "offended parties must fall to fighting. Their teeth, their nails, their feet, or fists, or, perhaps, the first club or stone that can be grasped, must decide the contest, by finishing the life of one." But the contest may not end with this death. "The father, the brother, or the friend, begins to espouse the cause of the deceased; not, indeed, so much from any love he bore him living, or from any grief he suffers for him dead, as from a principle of bravery and honor, to show himself able and willing to encounter the man who had just before vanquished another." From this arises the concept of "an avenger of blood."

Adams believed that the drive to personal vengeance was natural, nature having "implanted in the human heart a disposition to resent an injury when offered," a disposition "so strong, that even the horse treading by accident on a gouty toe, or a brickbat falling on the shoulders, in the first twinges of pain, seems to excite angry passions, and we feel an inclination to kill the horse and to break the brickbat." Whereas the French *philosophes* and their American followers, including Thomas Jefferson, saw humanity in a state of nature as uncorrupted and pure, Adams was far more wary. As he saw it, anything raw—natural—was neither inherently evil nor good, but both necessary and dangerous. Strength, force, power—all were necessary, but, uncontrolled, were at best useless and at worst destructive. Although he would agree with Jefferson and his ilk that certain rights were "natural," he did not believe that this implied the goodness of all that came directly from the Creator.

The instinct for personal vengeance, for example, was natural, even God-given, but to "exterminate from among mankind such revengeful sentiments and tempers," Adams wrote, "is one of the highest and most important strains of civil and humane policy." Government, he believed, should actively "suppress" all attempts at violently exacting personal vengeance. The alternative to simple vengeance was a concept of justice, which included social retribution and punishment, regulated, controlled, *managed*, and available only in civilized society, a group of human beings who have united for the common good.

The great project of Adams's life was reconciling natural rights with civilized society. Government, the highest form of management, was supposed to protect and preserve inalienable rights, those conferred by God or nature, yet also to control, regulate, and even suppress other aspects of humankind's heritage from God or nature, including, above all, the inherently antisocial instinct to personal vengeance. Management, including government, is not about liberating nature in the individual. It is not about creating a free man or woman, but about creating a free society—a union, an organization—of men and women. Whereas many others in the generation of John Adams, the generation of emerging revolutionaries, devoted themselves to securing individual liberties, Adams wrestled with the liberty of individuals united. It was a liberation from artificial tyranny as well as from the tyranny of nature. Individual liberty was at bottom bestial and brutish, an existence not worth preserving, whereas social liberty, life united in a commonwealth freely constituted, was not only worth building, but also defending and perpetuating.

**The Last Word:** Leaders of any commonwealth, whether national or corporate, must persuade every individual claiming a part in the enterprise that sacrifice is the only meaningful, enduring, and worthwhile means of gain. It is a paradox that runs contrary to common sense, that seems, in point of fact, unnatural, yet the essential truth of it derives from its very violation of common sense and its very distance from nature.

**Lesson 68**

## THE RIGHT TO KNOWLEDGE

*And liberty cannot be preserved without a general knowledge among the people.*

—*A Dissertation on the Canon and Feudal Law,* 1765

There can be no liberty without knowledge, Adams believed. As ignorance is the necessary climate for the growth of tyranny, so knowledge is necessary to nurture freedom. It is the duty of the leaders of a government to provide the means of educating the people, who "have a right, from the frame of their nature, to knowledge, as their great Creator, who does nothing in vain, has given them understandings, and a desire to know." Adams set the bar yet higher, declaring that the people have "an indisputable, unalienable, indefeasible, divine right to that most dreaded and envied kind of knowledge, I mean, of the characters and conduct of their rulers." The reason for this was that leadership, correctly conducted, was, as Adams saw it, a form of service. "Rulers are no more than attorneys, agents, and trustees, for the people." This being the case, the implication cannot be evaded that "if the cause, the interest and trust, is insidiously betrayed, or wantonly trifled away, the people have a right to revoke the authority that they themselves have deputed, and to constitute abler and better agents, attorneys, and trustees."

Since none of this could be carried out or upheld without popular knowledge, nothing in a government founded on liberty could be more important than education. "And the preservation of the means of knowledge among the lowest ranks, is of more importance to the public than all the property of all the rich men in the country." Moreover: "It is even of more consequence to the rich themselves, and to their posterity."

*Revolutionary Wisdom*
"Let every sluice of knowledge be opened and set a-flowing."
—A *Dissertation on the Canon and Feudal Law, 1765*

**The Last Word:** In any organization with ambition to prosper and endure, the great driver and end of stewardship must be education.

## Lesson 69
## FACTS ARE STUBBORN THINGS

*Facts are stubborn things, and whatever may be our wishes, our inclinations, or the dictums of our passions, they cannot alter the state of facts and evidence.*

—Closing argument to jury in the "Boston Massacre" trial,

December 5, 1770

John Adams, American revolutionary, leaped to the defense of the British redcoats charged with murder in the deaths of five Bostonians in the Boston Massacre. Their defense was hardly a popular cause; all Boston wanted the soldiers' blood. But Adams was convinced that no one in a free country could be denied a fair trial, and a fair trial required the assistance of able counsel.

Adams based his defense on self-defense, and it was brilliantly conducted. He was eloquent, yet he did not rely upon eloquence, but facts, which, in law, trump everything, including wishes, inclinations, and passions. Adams presented the facts, and all of the redcoats were spared the gallows. Of the officer and seven enlisted men tried, six were found not guilty and two were convicted not of murder but of manslaughter, for which they received the light—if painful—punishment of branding on the thumb.

Adams loved liberty and justice, which, in his view, were compatible only with absolute truth. If a nation aspired to liberty and justice, it must subordinate all passions, inclinations, and wishes to the truth of facts.

*Revolutionary Wisdom*

"We have entertained a great variety of phrases to avoid calling this sort of people a mob. Some call them shavers, some call them geniuses. The plain English is, gentlemen, it was most probably a motley rabble of saucy boys, Negroes and mulattoes, Irish teagues and outlandish jacktars. And why we should scruple to call such a people a mob, I can't conceive, unless the name is too respectable for them. The sun is not about to stand still or go out, nor the rivers to dry up because there was a mob in Boston on the 5th of March that attacked a party of soldiers. . . ."
—*Speech to the jury, "Boston Massacre" trial, December 3, 1770*

**The Last Word:** A leader makes many bargains, a multitude of compromises, but he never yields on the facts. Truth can never be regarded as a matter of mere convenience. It is either honored or destroyed. There is no middle ground.

## Lesson 70
## THE PERMANENCE OF PRINCIPLE

*Gravity is a principle of nature. Why? Because all particular bodies are found to gravitate. How would it sound to say, that bodies in general are heavy; yet to apply this to particular bodies, and say, that a guinea or a ball is heavy, is wild?*

—*Novanglus*, 1774–1775

"What are called revolution principles," John Adams wrote, were "the principles of Aristotle and Plato, of Livy and Cicero . . . the principles of nature and eternal reason." They are principles in nature in the same sense that gravity is "a principle in nature," and for that reason Adams found no basis on which to "insinuate a doubt concerning them." Yet many Americans did just that, arguing that while certain principles might be generally true, "the application of them to particular cases is wild and utopian." Adams could not accept this as a matter of logic. "How they can be in general true, and not applicable to particular cases, I cannot comprehend. I thought their being true in general, was because they were applicable in most particular cases." Gravity is generally true. So it must apply in the particular.

**The Last Word:** To identify a set of principles is to establish durable truth. To make a particular exception to a principle is to deny the validity of the principle or to deny the fact that the particular case presents. Leadership requires the integrity and courage to apply principle to every particular case.

**Lesson 71**
## A Family Value

*Fire them with ambition to be useful.*
>—Letter to Abigail, quoted in *John Adams* by David McCullough

Ambition, as Adams saw it, was quite literally a force of nature. Like everything else in nature, it was neither good nor bad in itself, but became good or bad depending how it was directed and used. Ambition could destroy a free society or it could build one. Whether it did the one or the other depended on how ambition was defined, and Adams believed that the definition needed to be made early in life. He was convinced that a free society began at the level of the family, and that it was the job of the family to inculcate in children the values necessary to win and maintain liberty. Thus, whereas most fathers might hope to "fire" their children with ambition to succeed or perhaps with ambition, period, Adams qualified his advice with the phrase "to be useful." His aim always was to integrate the individual into society. It was not that he sought selfless action and complete sacrifice, but that he was eager always to equate one's own good with that of the community or the nation.

**The Last Word:** An ambition to be "useful" implies working toward ends beyond yourself, yet ends that include yourself. Ambition thus defined ensures your own welfare within the context of what contributes to the community, whether this is your nation or your enterprise.

## Lesson 72
### A Declaration Delayed

*But on the other hand, the Delay of this Declaration to this Time, has many great Advantages attending it.*

—Letter to Abigail Adams, July 3, 1776

Managing any complex, high-stakes enterprise requires an exquisite sense of timing. The first letter John Adams wrote to Abigail on July 3, 1776—the day after the Declaration of Independence had been approved and the day before it was proclaimed—was filled with excitement and joy. A second letter, written later that same day, was afflicted by second thoughts. "Had a Declaration of Independency been made seven Months ago," Adams wrote, "it would have been attended with many great and glorious Effects," including (he believed) a host of powerful foreign alliances and possession of Canada.

Adams was never content to look at any achievement one-dimensionally, as an unalloyed good. The Declaration of Independence was a great thing—but it could have been so much greater, had it come earlier. Yet neither was he capable of looking at any reversal, failure, or disappointment as a one-dimensional disaster. "But on the other hand," he continued his second July 3 letter to Abigail Adams, "the Delay of this Declaration to this Time, has many great Advantages attending it.—The Hopes of Reconciliation, which were fondly entertained by Multitudes of honest and well meaning tho weak and mistaken People, have been gradually and at last totally extinguished."

**The Last Word:** In this letter, John Adams was uncharacteristically too optimistic in his assessment of unanimity on the subject of independence, but it was undeniably true that an increasing number of Americans now favored it. The most difficult commodity any leader must manage is time. It is both enemy and ally, stealing opportunity as well as providing it. Adams understood and accepted this calculus, but he also understood that it was not always strictly a matter of either/or, win/lose. On occasion, the passage of time yielded compensation for what it took away. "Time has been given for the whole People, maturely to consider the great Question of Independence and to ripen their Judgments, dissipate their Fears, and allure their Hopes, by discussing it in News Papers and Pamphletts, by debating it, in Assemblies, Conventions, Committees of Safety and Inspection, in Town and County Meetings, as well as in private Conversations." The great thing was not to allow regret to overtake action. The great thing was not to give up.

**Lesson 73**

CONSEQUENCES

---

*As their Act of Parliament would authorize them to try me in England for treason, and proceed to execution, too, I had no doubt they would go to the extent of their power, and practice upon me all the cruelties of their punishment of treason.*

—Manuscript autobiography, covering November 1777

When asked by the Continental Congress to serve as the nation's emissary to France, John Adams well knew that he would invite execution as a traitor if he were captured en route. Worse, his "family, consisting of a dearly beloved wife and four young children," filled him with "sentiments of tenderness, which a father and a lover only can conceive, and which no language can express." Such were the pressures to decline the commission. "On the other hand," he wrote, "my country was in deep distress and in great danger." He believed, moreover, that he was singularly well suited to the post, perhaps better suited than any other man. And so, "after much agitation of mind," Adams "resolved to devote my family and my life to the cause" and accepted the appointment.

**The Last Word:** Leadership requires sacrifice, the extent of which may well reach beyond oneself. Good leaders willingly make the sacrifices. The greatest leaders are those who make the sacrifices in the fullest and deepest understanding of what they are putting at stake.

**Lesson 74**

## GO THE WAY OF YOUR DUTY

*I thought myself in the way of my duty, and I did not repent of my voyage.*

—Diary, February 25, 1778

On February 15, 1778, John Adams embarked on the first ocean voyage of his life, bound for France as an emissary of the United States. The normal hazards of a winter Atlantic voyage were multiplied by making such a voyage in time of war. Subject to storms, Adams was also subject to attack, capture, trial for treason, and death by hanging.

The voyage was, for a fact, turbulent and stormy: "To describe the ocean, the waves, the winds; the ship, her motions, rollings, wringing, and agonies; the sailors, their countenances, language, and behavior, is impossible. No man could keep upon his legs, and nothing could be kept in its place; an universal wreck of every thing in all parts of the ship, chests, casks, bottles, &c. No place or person was dry." And as bad as this was, there was worse to come as the ship entered into what "are called the squally latitudes," which, Adams discovered, more than lived up to their name. "I should have been pleased to have kept a minute journal of all that passed . . . but I was so wet, and every thing and place was so wet, every table and chair was so wrecked, that it was impossible to touch a pen, or paper." Bruised, exhausted, profoundly seasick, Adams nevertheless observed that it was "a great satisfaction to me . . . to recollect that I was myself perfectly calm, during the whole." Everyone on the ship, the captain included, warned that the vessel was in "danger, and of this I was certain also, from my own observation; but I thought myself in the way of my duty, and I did not repent of my voyage."

**The Last Word:** As difficult as it may sometimes be to make a decision and to embark upon some high-stakes project, it is often even more difficult to sustain confidence, enthusiasm, and conviction when a project is in mid-course. Second thoughts can be both cruel and debilitating. In the end, what gets you through most reliably is a sense that you are acting "in the way of your duty." What you do for the sake of yourself in the context of your enterprise is always more compelling—and therefore more readily sustained—than what you do on your own account alone.

**Lesson 75**

Always Improve

*Have made many observations, in the late bad weather, . . . [a] few I will set down.*

—Diary, February 26, 1778

During the harrowing storms he experienced in his first voyage to Europe in February 1778 as an emissary of the United States, John Adams kept his eyes and ears open, making "many observations," including taking note of a number of ways in which his ship, the *Boston*, might be improved—or, at least, serve as an example to inspire the better design of new ships. He noted the "inexpressible inconvenience of having so small a space between decks," especially since, in the prevailing squall conditions, all ports and scuppers had to be kept closed, making it almost impossible to breathe below decks. He also observed that the ship was "over-metalled," carrying too many guns—too much weight—for her tonnage. He observed that the ship was "furnished with no pistols," a terrible deficiency, as he saw it, since "nothing but the dread of a pistol will keep many of the men to their quarters in time of action." Also absent were "good glasses"—telescopes—yet waste and a lack of economical practices were everywhere. Discipline, Adams believed, was generally lax. Cleanliness was neglected, and the volume of cursing was "silly as well as detestable." Meals were irregular, Adams complained, whereas there "ought to be a well digested system for eating, drinking, and sleeping," a precise routine that would promote "the health, comfort, and spirits of the men, and . . . greatly promote the business of the ship."

*Revolutionary Wisdom*

"It would be fruitless to attempt a description of what I saw, heard, and felt, during these three days and nights. To describe the ocean, the waves, the winds; the ship, her motions, rollings, wringing, and agonies; the sailors, their countenances, language, and behavior, is impossible. No man could keep upon his legs, and nothing could be kept in its place; an universal wreck of every thing in all parts of the ship, chests, casks, bottles, &c. No place or person was dry. On one of these nights, a thunderbolt struck three men upon deck, and wounded one of them a little by a scorch upon his shoulder; it also struck our maintop-mast."

—*Diary, February 23, 1778*

**The Last Word:** Seasick, storm-tossed, and in very real danger of losing his life, John Adams nevertheless made meticulous notes on what aspects of the young republic's naval routine could be redesigned and improved. A manager cannot help but manage.

**Lesson 76**

## The Source of Morality

*Could there be any morality left among such a people . . . ?*
—Manuscript autobiography, on the corruption of the French
government, when Adams was in Paris in 1778

The government with which John Adams dealt when he was one of America's ministers in France was so thoroughly corrupt and immoral that he asked himself whether there could be any morality left in the French people. "Yes," he answered. "There was a sort of morality. There was a great deal of humanity, and what appeared to me real benevolence." It was, however, all at the individual level. Simple human decency there was among the French, but it had failed to percolate up through the government, to become institutionalized. This was a great pity, Adams mused, but it was not a hopeless situation. "The foundations of national morality must be laid in private families," and, in France, he had seen that such foundations existed. It was a matter, somehow, of building on them.

**The Last Word:** Leadership is ultimately a bottom-up business. It begins with the values of individuals. Without this foundation, the organization cannot stand. Yet even in an enterprise consisting of ethical people, it remains the responsibility of the leaders, the managers, to draw those values into the organization as a whole, to raise the ethics of the enterprise on the foundation of individual values, deeply held rather than superficially applied. If emphasis is not laid upon personal ethics at the time of recruitment and hiring, these values may never become thoroughly integrated into the enterprise, and if they are not nurtured and rewarded on an ongoing basis, they will never pervade and inform the enterprise.

**Lesson 77**

# DIY

*I found that the Business of our Commission would never be done, unless
I did it.*

—Manuscript autobiography, regarding the negotiations
of alliance with the French, 1778

Sent by the Continental Congress as one of three commissioners
responsible for negotiating and managing an alliance with France,
Adams was appalled that his "two Colleagues would agree in nothing." He found the senior commissioner, the eminent Benjamin
Franklin, to be leading a life of what Adams characterized as "dis-
cipation" and complained that he "could never obtain the favour of
his Company in a Morning before Breakfast which would have been
the most convenient time to read over Letters and papers, deliberate
on their contents, and decide upon the Substance of the answers."
As for the other commissioner, Richard Henry Lee had grown even
more weary of Franklin than Adams had, and he now behaved with
a kind of sullen arrogance. The only solution Adams could think of
was to assume more responsibility and do the commission's work
himself.

**The Last Word:** Confronted with a choice between paralysis
and action, choose action.

**Lesson 78**

## THE FRUGAL MANAGER

*I determined to put my country to no further expense on my account.*
—Diary, April 10, 1778

Upon Adams's arrival outside Paris as one of the new republic's ministers to France, Benjamin Franklin, already installed there, showed the newcomer the "apartments and furniture left by" Silas Deane, Adams's predecessor. Adams found these in "every way more elegant than I desired," and although "Mr. Deane, in addition to these, had a house, furniture, and equipage, in Paris, I determined to put my country to no further expense on my account, but to take lodgings under the same roof with Dr. Franklin, and to use no other equipage than his, if I could avoid it."

John Adams was acutely aware that America was in a desperate financial struggle. High among the priorities of his European mission was the securing of loans and trade agreements to finance the revolution. These, he knew, would be matters of long and delicate negotiation. But there was something he himself could do immediately: live frugally, subjecting the nation to no unnecessary expense.

The Last Word: A good manager does whatever he can whenever he can do it.

## Lesson 79
## THE ONE, THE FEW, AND THE MANY

*You are afraid of the one—I, of the few. We agree perfectly that the many*
*should have a full and fair Representation.*
—Letter to Thomas Jefferson, December 6, 1787

Concerning the new Constitution being hammered out in Philadelphia, Thomas Jefferson worried that, by creating a strong executive branch, it risked transforming the American republic into a monarchy. Adams pointed out that the greatest danger was not from monarchy, but aristocracy. "You are Apprehensive of Monarchy; I, of Aristocracy," he wrote. "I would therefore have given more Power to the President and less to the Senate."

John Adams was less fearful that excessive or even absolute power would be assumed by any one man than he was that it would be usurped by a group, what he defined as an aristocracy. In his view, a single leader was less dangerous than a cabal or a conspiracy. Whereas an individual had to take responsibility for his actions, a group of individuals could hide behind the group. The situation of an aristocracy, which made power less responsible and less responsive to the people, was, in his view, far more corrosive to free, representative government than a situation approaching monarchy. It would, after all, be far easier to oust a single president than an entire Senate.

*Revolutionary Wisdom*
"But, as often as Elections happen, the danger of foreign Influence recurs. The less frequently they happen the less danger.
. . . Elections, my dear sir, Elections to offices which are great

objects of Ambition, I look at with terror. Experiments of this kind have been so often tryed, and so universally found productive of Horrors, that there is great Reason to dread them."
—*Letter to Thomas Jefferson, December 6, 1787*

**The Last Word:** With power should come great accountability. Yet it is accountability that is most elusive if great power is concentrated among a few rather than vested in a single leader. Management by committee often fails precisely because accountability in such a scheme is so hard to establish. Management by a monarch (one boss) may well be preferable to management by aristocracy (a committee). In any case, the belief that power apportioned among a few is any less absolute or any more representative than power vested in one is a dangerous delusion.

## Lesson 80
## PARTY LOYALTY

*If there are two candidates, each at the head of a party, the nation becomes divided into two nations, each of which is, in fact, a moral person, as much as any community can be so, and are soon bitterly enraged against each other.*

—*Discourses on Davila,* 1790–1791

Like George Washington, John Adams dreaded the creation of political parties. Unlike Washington, he became an enthusiastic member of one, the Federalist Party. Yet he understood the danger. It was not just that party loyalty might trump loyalty to the nation, but that each party would, in effect, become a collective person, thereby amplifying the effect of the passions that move individuals, too often at the expense of rational decision making.

While he accepted the creation of political parties as a fact—How could he do otherwise?—Adams never fully reconciled party and nation. Yet although he himself was instrumental in the creation of the Federalist Party, he was never blindly loyal to it. He soon found himself differing sharply from a faction that became known as the High Federalists, a wing led by Alexander Hamilton, who believed in the strong centralization of power. Hamilton's position constituted a renunciation of democracy that went too far even for Adams, and his split with the Hamiltonian faction cost him reelection to the presidency.

Parties—factions—seem to grow up naturally in organizations of all kinds. It is the manager's responsibility to monitor such developments and to ensure that nothing interrupts the connection between each member of the enterprise and the common good of the enterprise.

> *Revolutionary Wisdom*
> "The real terrors of both Parties have allways been, and now are, The fear that they shall loose the Elections and consequently the Loaves and Fishes; and that their Antagonists will obtain them. Both parties have excited artificial Terrors and if I were summoned as a Witness to say upon Oath, which Party had excited, Machiavillialy, the most terror, and which had really felt the most, I could not give a more sincere Answer, than in the vulgar Style 'Put Them in a bagg and shake them, and then see which comes out first.'"
> —*Letter to Thomas Jefferson, June 30, 1813*

**The Last Word:** Loyalty to a faction or a party is merely self-interest multiplied. It dilutes loyalty to the enterprise as a whole, and it presents a danger to effective management. Counteract factionalism by recognizing it when it develops and redirect the focus to common goals. Meetings, frank presentations, and strong direction are called for to prevent splintering.

## Lesson 81
## MANAGEMENT COP-OUTS

*I have read a great deal about the words fate and chance; but though I close my eyes to abstract my meditations, I never could conceive any idea of either.*

—Letter to John Taylor, April 15, 1814

John Taylor was a Virginian widely respected as a political thinker. In 1814, he wrote *An Inquiry into the Principles and Policy of the Government of the United States,* a long critique of Adams's own writings on government. The work stimulated a lively correspondence between Adams and Taylor.

Among the many charges Taylor leveled against Adams was that his "political system deduces government from a *natural* fate," whereas "the policy of the United States deduces it from *moral* liberty." In response, Adams denied the possibility of fate or chance as a true cause of anything. "When an action or event happens or occurs without a cause, some say it happens by chance," he wrote. "This is equivalent to saying that chance is no cause at all; it is nothing. Fate, too, is no cause, no agent, no power; it has no existence; it is not even a figment of imagination; it is a mere invention of a word without a meaning; it is a nonentity; it is nothing." He continued: "Liberty, according to my metaphysics, is an intellectual quality, an attribute that belongs not to fate nor chance. Neither possesses it, neither is capable of it."

*Revolutionary Wisdom*

"But America is a great, unwieldy Body. Its Progress must be slow. It is like a large Fleet sailing under Convoy. The fleetest Sailors must wait for the dullest and slowest. Like a Coach and six—the swiftest Horses must be slackened and the slowest quickened, that all may keep an even Pace...."

—*Letter to Abigail Adams, June 17, 1775*

**The Last Word:** John Adams would have enthusiastically applauded the plaque that famously stood on the Oval Office desk of Harry S. Truman: THE BUCK STOPS HERE. Like Truman, Adams was above all else unwilling to blame others for what he himself authored or, more generally, to ascribe any motive or cause to fate or chance. Verbal constructs that were otherwise nonentities, fate and chance constituted the ultimate cop-out, the most egregious passing of the buck. To resort to such a plea was a renunciation of authority as well as conscience, the antithesis of leadership and management.

# CHAPTER 6
## *Decision*

**Lesson 82**

SOME EQUATIONS OF LEADERSHIP

*Nature and truth, or rather truth and right are invariably the same in all times and in all places.*

—Diary, May 11, 1756

As a young attorney, John Adams accepted the reality that different people had differing perspectives on the truth, but, unlike many modern philosophers, he rejected the notion that truth, therefore, was a relative commodity, a product, in effect, of perspective. For him, truth was an absolute, the equivalent of nature, which in turn was the equivalent of right; therefore, truth and right were also equivalent: "the same in all times and in all places." This equation, he believed, was self-evident to "reason, pure unbiased reason"; the problem, however, was that "passion, prejudice, interest, custom, and fancy" often "blinded or perverted" our understanding, prompting us to "embrace errors." From these defects in our understanding arose "that endless variety of opinions entertained by mankind."

One of the leader's most important responsibilities, as Adams saw it, was to exclude bias and all the other factors that pollute "pure reason." This was no easy task, but the existence of law was an invaluable aid to it. Standing apart from "passion, prejudice, interest, custom, and fancy," law functioned to keep people focused on unchanging truth, right, and nature.

*Revolutionary Wisdom*

"The reasoning of mathematicians is founded on certain and infallible principles. Every word they use conveys a determinate idea, and by accurate definitions they excite the same ideas in the mind of the reader that were in the mind of the writer. When they have defined the terms they intend to make use of, they premise a few axioms, or self-evident principles, that every man must assent to as soon as proposed. They then take for granted certain postulates, that no one can deny ... and from these plain simple principles they have raised most astonishing speculations, and proved the extent of the human mind to be more spacious and capable than any other science."

—*Diary, June 1, 1756*

**The Last Word:** For many of us today, adopting Adams's absolutism with regard to the nature of truth may not be possible. That does not mean, however, that the leader of any enterprise must uncritically embrace relativism. Use the equivalent of law to establish a firm ethical and business basis for your enterprise, a set of policies and principles defined as absolute, a lodestone not subject to the "passion, prejudice, interest, custom, and fancy" of any individual or set of individuals. Invite, admit, allow, and evaluate the entire range of opinion and interpretation within your organization, but, in the end, ground judgment, decision, and choice in principle.

**Lesson 83**

## The Decision to Oppose

*The steady management of a good government is the most anxious, arduous, and hazardous vocation on this side of the grave.*
—"On Self-Delusion," *Boston Gazette,* August 1763

John Adams was a revolutionary, not a rabble-rouser. In his second published essay, "On Self-Delusion," he warned his countrymen not to allow themselves to "be bubbled . . . out of our reverence and obedience to government on the one hand; nor out of our right to think and act for ourselves in our own department on the other." Making a revolution was not to be taken lightly, but that did not mean abandoning revolution. Still, managing a good government was very hard and very risky work, and it was folly to "encumber those . . . who have spirit enough to embark in such an enterprise, with any kind of opposition that the preservation or perfection of our mild, our happy, our most excellent constitution, does not soberly demand." A revolution should not be fought over trifles, including some transitory dissatisfaction. Only if basic rights—those guaranteed by the body of law and tradition commonly referred to as the British "constitution"—were ill-served by the government or directly violated by it was revolution not only justified, but soberly demanded.

**The Last Word:** The management of any complex enterprise in which a multitude of stakeholders clamor for satisfaction is anxious, arduous, and hazardous, and therefore not to be casually criticized. But when leadership fails in the fundamentals, revolution figures not as an option, but a sober demand. The alternative is the collapse of the enterprise.

**Lesson 84**

FEAR

---

*The true source of our sufferings has been our timidity. We have been afraid to think.*

—*A Dissertation on the Canon and Feudal Law,* 1765

Fear is the ally and enabler of tyrants. Faced with the outrage of the Stamp Act, taxation without representation, many people, Adams observed, hesitated to examine and consider "the grounds of our privileges, and the extent in which we have an indisputable right to demand them, against all the power and authority on earth."

Fear is the enemy of knowledge. And indeed, Adams acknowledged the danger of challenging tyranny. Although this danger did not nullify the right to demand all unalienable rights, such a demand had to be made "against all the power and authority on earth"—a most daunting prospect. Dangerous, daunting—yes. But the alternative, timid submission to tyranny, was even more dangerous, because it was the road to slavery.

**The Last Word:** *A hard lesson in leadership*—Doing the right thing is sometimes both dangerous *and* the only viable course of action. Knowledge can be hazardous, but ignorance will not save you. Survival is not always easy, but it is preferable to the alternative.

## Lesson 85
## A CAUSE FOR REVOLUTION?

*"In the political compact, the smallest defect in the prince a revolution."*
*By no means; but a manifest design in the prince.*

*—Novanglus, 1774–1775*

"Massachusettensis," the pseudonymous anti-independence politi-cal pamphleteer in opposition to whom Adams wrote *Novanglus,* held that the leaders of rebellion in New England were inciting revolution over "the smallest defect in the prince." Adams countered that the object was not a mere defect, small or great, but a "mani-fest design," which was aimed at annulling the king's "contract" with his people. Adams held that, as long as King George III extended his protection to the colonies, they did indeed owe him allegiance. When, however, George moved to consign colonial administra-tion to a Parliament in which the colonists had no representation, the king annulled the contract, and the bonds between Britain and America were dissolved, replaced by a "settled plan to deprive the people of all the benefits, blessings, and ends of the contract, to sub-vert the fundamentals of the constitution, to deprive them of all share in making and executing laws." This, Adams wrote, was ample reason to "justify a revolution."

**The Last Word:** Profound and consequential actions require profound and consequential grounds. It is often dangerous to allow a single event to determine a course of action. Pattern, design, and evidence of intention are far more reliable indicators of the real-ity of a situation and therefore make more compelling and certain incentives to any high-stakes decision.

**Lesson 86**
NOTHING TO LOSE

*They can hardly be losers if unsuccessful. . . . If they succeed, their gains are immense.*

—*Novanglus*, 1774–1775

The most compelling disincentive to action is the possibility of losing by that action. Adams sought to precipitate revolution by persuading his countrymen that they had, in fact, nothing to lose. To the assertion of "Massachusettensis" that "the people are sure to be losers in the end," Adams responded that if they were unsuccessful but lived, "they can but be slaves . . . and slaves they would have been, if they had not resisted." Nothing, therefore, would be lost. "If they die, they cannot be said to lose, for death is better than slavery." But if "they succeed, their gains are immense. They preserve their liberties."

**The Last Word:** No argument is more compelling than nothing-to-lose/everything-to-gain. Just be certain that you can make the argument honestly and persuasively. Use it if you can.

**Lesson 87**

## PASSIVITY

*The author of a "Friendly Address to all reasonable Americans" . . . pronounce[s] damnation . . . on all who practice implicit, passive obedience to an established government, of whatever character it may be.*

—*Novanglus*, 1774–1775

Revolution is dangerous, but far more dangerous is passive obedience to a government for the sole reason that it is "established" and without regard to its "character." Such passivity is fundamentally irrational.

**The Last Word:** Often, a leader's most difficult task is to persuade others that inaction presents a greater risk than action. We naturally tend to believe that we are safest with the status quo. But what if the status quo is destructive? In such a case, passivity can be fatal—certainly without sense, and quite possibly crazy. At times, it is urgently necessary to shake an organization out of its complacency. The first step is to challenge the assumption that we must accept what is established because it is established. For many, such a challenge will come as a profound revelation.

**Lesson 88**

## Promote Change with Precedent

*The practice of nations has been different.*

—*Novanglus*, 1774–1775

In 1774, part of America was a British colony and had been for more than a century and a half. This was established reality, and established reality is heavily freighted with inertia. To overcome this inertia, Adams applied a reality even more established. He wrote that "there is nothing in the law of nations, which is only the law of right reason applied to the conduct of nations, that requires that emigrants from a state should continue, or be made, a part of the state." To promote this assertion against established fact, he turned to established fact: "The practice of nations has been different [from that of Britain with regard to America]," he wrote. "The Greeks planted colonies, and neither demanded nor pretended any authority over them; but they became distinct, independent commonwealths. The Romans continued their colonies under the jurisdiction of the mother commonwealth; but, nevertheless, they allowed them the privileges of cities. . . . It was the policy of Rome to conciliate her colonies by allowing them equal liberties with her citizens." Independence from the mother country was no innovation, but literally ancient history.

**The Last Word:** For any established, ongoing enterprise, change is simultaneously inviting and frightening. Sell change by means of precedent. Emphasize the benefits of the new, but demonstrate its continuity with the familiar. Effective managers define revolution not as a break with the past but as an accelerated evolution from it.

**Lesson 89**

DELEGATING

*Your commission constitutes you commander of all the forces . . . and you are vested with full power and authority to act as you shall think for the good and welfare of the service.*

—Letter to General George Washington, 1776

It was John Adams who nominated George Washington as commander in chief of the newly created Continental Army. At the time of its creation, this force was known as the Boston Army and surrounded the British garrison in that city. Pondering what should come next after action in Boston, Washington wrote to Adams to ask if his command authority extended to mounting a defense of New York. The very essence of Adams's philosophy was the careful monitoring and regulation of power and authority. Nevertheless, he knew when to delegate power and authority in absolute terms. He knew when to abandon the monitoring and second guessing. With confidence in Washington's courage, judgment, and military skill, Adams assured Washington that his command was limited only by his own sense of what was for "the good and welfare of the service."

**The Last Word:** The most important step in delegating authority is recruitment. Devote the effort necessary to getting people in whom you can invest full confidence—then invest it, unambiguously. The time for pondering and second thoughts is at the stage of recruitment and evaluation, not at the point of execution.

**Lesson 90**
## WORTH WINNING

*Yet through all the Gloom I can see the Rays of ravishing Light and Glory.*
—Letter to Abigail Adams, July 3, 1776

No one who knew John Adams would have accused him of blind optimism. Nor was he a pessimist. Quick to see opportunity, Adams was almost as quick to see the liabilities within any opportunity. But he was never paralyzed by this dual vision, not when he saw something worth winning. To Abigail, he wrote on July 3, 1776: "You will think me transported with Enthusiasm but I am not.—I am well aware of the Toil and Blood and Treasure, that it will cost us to maintain this Declaration [of Independence], and support and defend these States." What sustained him through this recognition of liability was a vision of the "Rays of ravishing Light and Glory" that lay beyond. "I can see," he wrote, "that the End is more than worth all the Means." Though we may from time to time have reason to regret the Declaration, to "rue it," Adams was confident "that Posterity will tryumph" as a result of it.

**The Last Word:** The vision of leadership never fails to acknowledge dangers, costs, and liabilities, but it does not stop with these. Instead, it looks through them to the ends that are worth winning.

## Lesson 91
### Consequences of Cross-Purposes

*... Obstructions, Embarrassments and studied Delays ...*
—Letter to Abigail Adams, July 3, 1776

As if taking on the world's greatest military power to win the independence of the lower thirteen American colonies were not sufficiently audacious, the Continental Congress, early in the Revolution, authorized an expedition to conquer Canada. Not surprisingly, it failed disastrously. In a letter to his wife, Abigail, John Adams attributed the defeat to conflicting motives among the American strategists. While many had hoped for success, Adams knew that "Others there are in the Colonies who really wished our Enterprise in Canada would be defeated, that the Colonies might be brought into Danger and Distress between two Fires, and be thus induced to submit" to the mother country. No one understood better than John Adams that the people of the colonies had entered the revolution hardly united in their desire for independence. Months before the Declaration of Independence was finally adopted, Adams estimated that as much as a third of the country was against independence and perhaps another third was either indifferent to it or ambivalent about it. Yet, with regard to the Canadian debacle, that was not the worst of it. Even among those who were ambivalent, Adams recognized some who "really wished to defeat the Expedition ... lest the conquest of [Canada] should elevate the Minds of the People too much to hearken to those Terms of Reconciliation which they believed would be offered Us." In other words, some feared that a Patriot conquest of Canada would carry the Revolution beyond the point of any possible resolution. It was, Adams wrote, a collection of "jarring Views, Wishes and Designs [that] caused Obstructions, Embarrassments and studied Delays, which have finally, lost Us the Province."

John Adams had been in the forefront of those who agitated for revolution in order to bring about complete independence from England. He believed there was no compromise, reconciliation, or middle course possible because the colonies could never be properly represented in Parliament and, therefore, could never be attached to the mother country by any bond other than tyranny. He understood that his conviction was not universal, and he set out to persuade a sufficient number to create a kind of critical mass in favor of independence. He never believed that he or anyone else would be able to sway the entire country. Yet events unfolded before even that critical mass had been achieved. At Lexington and Concord on April 19, 1775, the fighting began, even though the Patriots had not agreed on independence or any other war aim. Adams and others in the pro-independence faction scrambled to bring their issue to the fore, yet, even at the time of the Canadian venture, there was a range of opinion and sentiment sufficiently broad and contradictory to fatally cripple the boldest Patriot offensive of the war.

**The Last Word:** The American Revolution survived the Canadian debacle—barely. But there is no easy lesson to be derived from the ill-conceived expedition. The hard fact is that decisive action cannot always wait upon unanimity. Indeed, most of the time, in most organizations, the best a leader can hope for is to achieve a critical mass of buy-in and collective will sufficient to drive an action successfully. Once success has been achieved, the rest of the organization will probably buy in as well. The decision to act, however, is by nature a calculated risk, and the consequences of cross-purposes in any high-stakes action are potentially fatal. Consciousness of this reality is among the heaviest burdens of leadership.

**Lesson 92**

Managing Independence

*. . . to be completely independent . . .*

—Diary, October 11, 1782

The Battle of Yorktown, concluded on October 19, 1781, ended for all practical purposes the American Revolution. Yet the great task remained to negotiate a full and formal treaty. With John Jay and Benjamin Franklin, John Adams served as the key negotiator. In this role, he quickly perceived that the interests of the United States were hardly uppermost in the minds of either the British or the French treaty commissioners, and he noted that "it was easy to foresee that France and England both would endeavor to involve us in their future wars." Having fought to win independence, Adams intended to negotiate a treaty that would guarantee that independence in the fullest and most absolute sense. "I thought America had been long enough a foot-ball between contending nation, and . . . I thought it our interest and duty to . . . be completely independent, and have nothing to do, but in commerce, with either" France or England. From the beginning, Adams noted, "my thoughts had been . . . constantly employed to arrange all our European connections to this end."

**The Last Word:** Define clear and unambiguous goals and use them as lenses to focus all activity toward achieving them. Measure success by how closely you hit your target. Identify those goals that may be subject to negotiation and those that are non-negotiable and must be attained entire and intact.

**Lesson 93**

## Bolster Theory with History

*There is no example of a government simply democratical.*
— *A Defence of the Constitutions of the United States of America*, 1789

John Adams had more than liberty to promote. He had a theory of government to sell—the three-branched system, including a bicameral legislature, proposed in the new Constitution, which was in process of ratification when he wrote his *Defence* of this national document as well as the several constitutions already adopted by the states. Many, both within the United States and abroad, objected that the three-branch government and, especially, the bicameral legislature were too complex and tended to dilute what they thought should be an absolute American democracy. As Adams had used historical precedent to foment, organize, and support the revolution, so now he used it to lend support to the shaping of the post-Revolutionary government.

Nowhere in history, he argued, did a "simply democratical" government exist. Indeed, "from the history of all the ancient republics of Greece, Italy, and Asia Minor, as well as from those that still remain in Switzerland, Italy, and elsewhere," Adams wrote, it may be concluded that "caprice, instability, turbulence, revolutions, and the alternate prevalence of those two plagues and scourges of mankind, tyranny and anarchy, were the effects of government without three orders [branches] and a balance." The whole of the *Defence*, three full volumes written between 1786 and 1789, is a remarkable and vast historical survey of republican governments from ancient Greece to the eighteenth century, each word aimed at supporting the necessity of a three-branched government with a bicameral legislature by showing the consequences of republican government lacking these.

> *Revolutionary Wisdom*
> "I always consider the settlement of America with reverence and wonder, as the opening of a grand scene and design in providence, for the illumination of the ignorant and the emancipation of the slavish part of mankind all over the earth."
> —*Adams's notes for* A Dissertation on the Canon and Feudal Law, *1765*

**The Last Word:** Called upon to accept change, people crave data, historical evidence suggesting that the proposed innovation will work and will not result in catastrophe. Leadership for change does not rest on the theoretical formulation of innovation, but builds a persuasive case upon historical data, the more overwhelming the more persuasive.

**Lesson 94**

## Real Merit

---

*[R]eal merit is confined to a very few, [and] the numbers who thirst for respect, are out of all proportion to those who seek it only by merit.*
—*Discourses on Davila*, 1790–1791

Although "no appetite in human nature is more universal than that for honor," Adams wrote, "real merit" is remarkably scarce because the "great majority trouble themselves little about merit," but instead seek "honor"—attention, notoriety, fame. To do this, they use "artifice, dissimulation, hypocrisy, flattery" and even outright "bribery." It is not entirely the fault of those who seek honor. The fact is, Adams argued, that "Real merit is . . . remote from the knowledge of whole nations," largely because of sheer numbers; after all, "no individual [is] personally known to an hundredth part of the nation." This means that real merit cannot speak with nearly so loud a voice as does fame.

The difficulty of recognizing real merit and therefore the difficulty of putting into positions of power and authority those individuals who possess it is a major problem of democratic government. "The voters . . . must be exposed to deception . . . chicanery, impostures and falsehoods."

How to solve the problem? Adams observed that many nations "have sought for something more permanent than the popular voice to designate honor." These means have included restricting power to those who own great estates or who belong to "great families." The problem with this, Adams argued, was the tendency to create "aristocratical anarchy," the placement of people in positions of power based on terms at least as arbitrary as popular election and, therefore, at least as unlikely to distinguish real merit. Adams suggested combining popular election with appointment by a select few. This plan was reflected in his proposal for a bicameral legislature, consisting of a popularly elected lower house and an essentially appointed upper house. Adams did not claim that this ensured selection on the basis of real merit, but it improved the odds.

Managers face a similar problem. On the one hand, there is a desire to include a large segment of the organization in selecting team leaders and supervisors, but, on the other, a concern that doing so will degenerate into a mere popularity contest. Public opinion, after all, is not always correct. Yet the extreme alternative of making unilateral appointments is not always the best way to ensure that those with real merit are put in positions of power. Subordinates are often in a better position to judge merit than managers are. Moreover, there is a decided morale and motivational advantage in giving the rank and file a voice in management at least at the level that most immediately affects them. The best course is to retreat from either extreme, neither relinquishing all authority to the organization nor unilaterally assuming it, but instead soliciting opinions, conducting good-faith forums, and then using the results of these to make an informed management decision.

**The Last Word:** In most organizations, employees do not want management to relinquish decision authority to them, but they do want their opinions heard and considered. What is more, these opinions provide a valuable perspective on the running of the enterprise. They should not be ignored or squandered.

**Lesson 95**
## The Power of Prophecy

*The Crusades were commenced by the Prophets and every Age since, when ever any great Turmoil happens in the World, has produced fresh Prophets. The Continual Refutation of all their Prognostications by Time and Experience has no Effect in extinguishing or damping their Ardor.*
—Letter to Thomas Jefferson, February 10, 1812

Soothsayers, sages, and gurus are popular in every age, no matter that their predictions fail to come to pass. Never mind that "Time and Experience" consistently discredit them, they exercise a charismatic hold on the mass of people.

Prediction is a key leadership function. In the simplest sense of the word, a *leader* leads. That means he is at the front. He looks ahead and is supposed to see what's coming, then lead his followers accordingly. No wonder prophecy offers such a powerful seduction.

**The Last Word:** Base prediction on observation and extrapolation, on present fact and on the imagination of future fact thoroughly grounded in the present. Do not rely on persuasive personalities to supply a vision of the future. Just as disputes should be settled through an unblinking focus on issues rather than a blurry picture of personalities, so the anticipation of the future must be built out from a foundation of real data rather than opinion, no matter how powerfully presented.

**Lesson 96**

## The Gap of Knowing

*Knowledge cannot always accompany events.*
—Letter to John Taylor, April 15, 1814

"I hope it will be no offence to say, that public opinion is often formed upon imperfect, partial, and false information from the press. Public information cannot keep pace with facts." Indeed, Adams observed, "Knowledge cannot always accompany events."

For Adams, the implication of this assessment was that, ideally, the leaders of a government should possess the ability to bridge what we might call "the gap of knowing" more effectively than the general public. In an age before mass communication, this was more easily done than it is now—although the gap of knowing was wider for leaders as well as the general public. Today, knowledge is distributed far more democratically. The challenge posed by the leveling of knowledge, whether in government or business, is for leaders to obtain data of the highest quality and accuracy. Often, this is a matter of source as well as selection. In our heavily mediated culture, we swim in a world of information, and reducing the gap of knowing is as much a process of filtering—selecting only the best and most useful data, while rejecting the rest—as it is of gathering.

*Revolutionary Wisdom*
"Your Speculations into Futurity in Europe are so probable that I can suggest no doubts to their disadvantage. All will depend on the Progress of Knowledge. But how shall Knowledge Advance? Independent of Temporal and Spiritual Power, the Course of Science and Literature is obstructed

and discouraged by so many Causes that it is to be feared, their motions will be slow."

—*Letter to Thomas Jefferson, February 2, 1816*

## The Last Word: Adams was right. Despite our best efforts, knowledge cannot always accompany events. Your task as a manager is to do your best to synchronize events and knowledge, but when this cannot be achieved, the best course may be one of restraint, delaying important decisions until you are confident that you have good information, that knowledge has caught up with the event. In many pressing situations, the exercise of such restraint is a singularly demanding test of leadership.

**Lesson 97**
## The Truth About Teams

*Make all men Newtons, or, if you will, Jeffersons, or Taylors, or Randolphs, and they would all perish in a heap!*
—Letter to John Taylor, April 15, 1814

"The constant labor of nine tenths of our species will forever be necessary to prevent all of them from starving with hunger, cold, and pestilence," John Adams observed. If everyone in a society were a genius, a great thinker, an important philosopher, who would do the actual work? A society, a nation—any organized enterprise— requires the contributions of people of diverse abilities and interests: planners and workers, managers and subordinates.

Most managers will readily accept this as a common-sense truth. Yet, when it comes time to create a work group or a project team, these very managers will scour the enterprise for the "most creative" people and pack the team with them. The result? More often than not, the team gets stuck. It begins well, with ideas flowing in abundance. But because everyone on board is "creative," the team's output rarely gets beyond the stage of idea and into that of implementation.

The truth is that, stocked with nothing but creative geniuses, a team will fail to produce—or, at least, to produce anything more than ideas, than beginnings. Any group tasked with producing tangible results requires diversity in its composition. In addition to creative types, a productive team requires people who are good at developing what the creators create. It needs other people who approach ideas analytically and critically, who question whether an idea can be made to work. And, finally, a productive team requires members who may not be very good at originating ideas, but who know how to implement them, how to get things done, how to get ideas produced, and how to keep the whole process running.

*Revolutionary Wisdom*

"To come to our own country, and to the times when you and I became first acquainted, we well remember the violent parties which agitated the old Congress, and their bitter contests. There you and I were together, and the Jays, and the Dickinsons, and other anti-independants were arrayed against us. They cherished the monarchy of England; and we the rights of our countrymen. When our present government was in the mew, passing from Confederation to Union, how bitter was the schism between the Feds and the Antis. Here you and I were together again."

—*Thomas Jefferson, letter to John Adams, June 27, 1813*

**The Last Word:** In most organizations, the creative geniuses are favored and maybe even most highly rewarded. They are, however, neither more nor less valuable than people who can develop ideas, people who can constructively criticize ideas, and people who can find and tighten the nuts and bolts necessary to transform ideas into reality.

CHAPTER 7

# *Reality*

## Lesson 98

### LAW OF CHANGE

*All that part of Creation that lies within our observation is subject to change.*

—Letter to cousin and Harvard classmate Nathan Webb,
October 12, 1755

"Even mighty states and kingdoms are not exempted" from what Adams described as a law or principle of change. "Immortal Rome was at first but an insignificant village . . . but by degrees it rose to a stupendous height," only to fall in due course: "But the demolition of Carthage (what one should think should have established it in supreme domination) by removing all danger, suffered it to sink into debauchery, and made it at length an easy prey to Barbarians." The fall of Rome, in its turn, enabled the "increase" of England "in power and magnificence," so that it "is now the greatest nation upon the globe." Yet the "few people" who came from England to America "for conscience sake," Adams wrote, may well have set the stage for the "transfer . . . of empire into America," which, "in another century, [will] become more [populous] than England itself." This eventuality will ensure that even "the united force of all Europe . . . will not be able to subdue us." Indeed, the "only way to keep us from setting up for ourselves"—becoming an independent nation—"is to disunite us," to "[k]eep us in distinct colonies," so that "some great men in each colony, desiring the monarchy of the whole, . . . will destroy each others' influence and keep the country in *equilibrio*."

This extraordinary vision of the future, outlined to a cousin and college chum in 1755, twenty years before Lexington and Concord, is important not only as a remarkable prediction of revolution and independence and of how early these ideas formed in the mind of John Adams, but also of his conception of revolution not as some exceptional event in the source of history, but as a function of something very much like natural law.

Everything, Adams believed, is subject to change. Like other forces of nature, however, change was in itself morally neutral. It could produce good or ill. It could reform or corrupt, create or destroy. It was the responsibility of each generation to control and direct change. If America was to emerge, because of population growth, as greater than its mother country, then it was up to the current generation to create a union sufficient to withstand the "united force of all Europe" so that the Americans might form themselves into an independent nation. This was by no means inevitable. If Americans were disunited, so that "great men" in the various colonies would contend with one another for supremacy of the whole, then the colonial status quo would likely endure, and America, no matter how populous and powerful it became, would remain an appendage of England.

**The Last Word:** The manager who relies exclusively on some principle or law to effect desired change makes the fatal error of abrogating leadership. Management is synonymous with control, and control is lost once the enterprise is relinquished to forces outside of itself. Recognize, acknowledge, and define the precedents, trends, and principles that influence your business. Exploit them, gain inspiration and direction from them, but do not surrender to them.

**Lesson 99**

## STABILITY IS NOWHERE TO BE FOUND

*Why am I so unreasonable as to expect happiness, and a solid, undisturbed contentment, amidst all the disorders and the continual rotations of worldly affairs?*

—Diary, August 14, 1756

Casting his eye and mind about him one summer morning in 1756, John Adams concluded that "Stability is nowhere to be found in that part of the universe that lies within our observation; the natural and the moral world are continually changing . . ." Not only do the planets orbit and whirl, "the clouds gather, the winds rise, lightnings glare, and thunders bellow," but man himself "is sometimes flushed with joy, and transported with the full fury of sensual pleasure" yet "the next hour lies groaning under the bitter pangs of disappointment and adverse fortune."

The object of government is the same as that of management. It is the introduction of stability within change, within advance, within process. But where in the world, Adams asked, was such stability to be found? Surely not "in that part of the universe that lies within our observation." Where, then? Adams believed it was to be found in "a state of moral discipline," which encompassed (for him) "habits of virtue, self-government, and piety." For a "world in flames, and a whole system tumbling in ruins to the centre, have nothing terrifying in them to a man whose security is builded on the adamantine basis of good conscience and confirmed piety."

*Revolutionary Wisdom*

"I would recommend it to you to become acquainted with the history of that country [Holland], as in many respects it is similar to the Revolution of your own. Tyranny and oppression were the original causes of the revolt of both countries. It is from a wide and extensive view of mankind that a just and true estimate can be formed of the powers of human nature."
—*Abigail Adams, letter to John Quincy Adams, May 26, 1781*

**The Last Word:** No active enterprise is truly stable. Business creates, responds, incites, tears down, consumes, and produces. Business is continual change. Physical stability is the death of business, and yet to surrender to the flux of commerce is also fatal, a "world in flames, and a whole system tumbling in ruins to the centre." Whatever else a manager does, she must be keeper, defender, and administrator of the enduring and collective values of the enterprise. Leadership brings stability to the active organization by maintaining the guiding principles of that organization, the equivalent of Adams's "adamantine basis" of virtue, self-government, conscience, and piety.

**Lesson 100**

REPUTATION

---

*Reputation ought to be the perpetual subject of my thoughts, and aim of my behavior. How shall I gain a reputation?*

—Diary, March 14, 1759

Early in life, John Adams turned inward, concluding that one's identity lay within and that the perceptions and opinions of others were inherently changeable and often wildly unstable. As he entered into the public arena through the practice of law, however, he came to realize that his identity could not be defined entirely within himself, that it required at least partial definition by society. This is what was meant by "reputation." Shakespeare's Roderigo said it in *Othello*: "Reputation, reputation, reputation! O! I have lost my reputation. I have lost the immortal part of myself, and what remains is bestial."

As Adams understood it, reputation is what would enable him to make a mark on the world—first as a lawyer and then as a leader. But how to acquire a reputation without upsetting the balance between his inner, self-defined identity—his deepest moral self— and the expectation of others?

He wondered whether he should "make frequent visits in the neighborhood, and converse familiarly with men, women, and children, in their own style," focusing on the "common tittle-tattle of the town," but taking "every fair opportunity of showing my knowledge in the law." Or should he renew his acquaintance with the now-prominent "young gentlemen in Boston who were at college with me"? The problem with both of these approaches to reputation building was that they were time-consuming and would "require more art . . . and patience . . . than I am master of." This being the case, Adams thought, perhaps he should concentrate on impressing other lawyers, endeavoring "to get a great character for understanding and learning with them." The problem with this approach was the effect of the inevitable "envy, jealousy, and self-interest" prevailing in the profession. Would it be better, then, to acquire rapid fame by finding "a cause to speak to, and exert all the soul and all the body I own, to cut a flash, strike amazement, to catch the vulgar"?

In the end, Adams found no ready answer, except to "assume a fortitude, a greatness of mind." He had identified early on the problem of any principled person who wanted to assume a position of prominence. The self-containment and integrity of self-definition were impossible to sustain in a position that called for answering to the needs and desires of the people in order to lead them.

**The Last Word:** A leader must, in some measure, define himself in response to those he leads. But to do this wholeheartedly would be to relinquish rather than acquire a true identity. "I feel vexed, fretted, and chafed," Adams complained to his diary. Any thoughtful leader would. Building an effective, enduring, responsive, yet authentic reputation is the great project of fashioning oneself into the role of leader. It is a project of inordinate difficulty, and it is one that must be carried forward but that can never be completed.

**Lesson 101**
## A WORD OF ADVICE

*Let them consider how extremely addicted they are to magnify and exaggerate the injuries that are offered to themselves, and to diminish and extenuate the wrongs that they offer to others.*
—"On Private Revenge, No. III," *Boston Gazette*, September 5, 1763

If there was to be a revolution, John Adams wanted a just revolution, which meant a revolution entirely divorced from any personal motives. He admonished the readers of his essay "On Private Revenge, No. III" "to look into their own hearts, which they will find to be deceitful above all things and desperately wicked." He did not mean that human beings were inherently evil, but that their emotions, unchecked and unexamined, provided unreliable promptings to decisive action.

Humanity as a species, Adams believed, was prone to magnify injuries received and minimize injuries dealt. This common infirmity called for people to be "too modest and diffident of their own judgment, when their own passions and prejudices and interests are concerned, to desire to judge for themselves in their own causes, and to take their own satisfactions for wrongs and injuries of any kind." Vengeance—action in redress of wrong—should be conceived and evaluated in rational, principled terms, not in accordance with the heat of one's heart.

**The Last Word:** Calibrate action to reality itself, not to the emotions reality produces. Overreacting to a perceived injury may well produce the injury in fact.

**Lesson 102**

QUESTION AUTHORITY

*Discovery, if that was incontestable, could give no title to the English king, by common law, or by the law of nature, to the lands, tenements, and hereditar~ents of the native Indians here.*

—*Novanglus,* 1774–1775

Great Britain claimed sovereignty over America by virtue of having discovered and settled parts of it. Seeking to undermine all basis for British rule in America, Adams examined the claim and found it wanting. "How, in common sense," he asked, "came the dominions of King Philip, King Massachusetts, and twenty other [Native American] sovereigns, independent princes here, to be within the allegiance of the Kings of England, James and Charles? America was no more within the allegiance of those princes, by the common law of England, or by the law of nature, than France and Spain were." What is more, Adams introduced historical evidence that "our ancestors were sensible of this," as revealed by the fact that they "honestly purchased their lands of the natives."

The Last Word: Do not let your opponents define the terms of an argument. Instead, question authority by challenging the assumptions on which authority rests. You may find those assumptions to be unwarranted and the field, therefore, wide open to you.

**Lesson 103**

## THE LIMIT OF PERSUASION

*I appeal to all experience, and to universal history, if it has ever been in the power of popular leaders, uninvested with other authority than what is conferred by the popular suffrage, to persuade a large people, for any length of time together, to think themselves wronged, injured, and oppressed, unless they really were, and saw and felt it to be so.*

*—Novanglus, 1774–1775*

To those who protested that the American Patriots were nothing more than rabble-rousers, malcontents who filled the people with an unwarranted desire for rebellion, Adams answered that the power of persuasion was limited. He contended that a leader could only persuade a large number of people of a thing over a sustained period if that thing were actually true. The point is subject to much debate. John Adams, after all, was unfamiliar with the likes of Adolf Hitler and Joseph Stalin. Yet there can be little doubt that, under ordinary circumstances, a fiction is far more difficult to sustain than the truth.

**The Last Word:** Persuasive management cannot be built upon lies or errors, but must be conducted within the parameters of fact. Encountering sustained resistance is a signal to reexamine your perception of the situation and your interpretation of the facts.

**Lesson 104**

## ALL BUSINESS IS PEOPLE BUSINESS

*The nation, I believe, is not vindictive, but the minister has discovered himself to be so in a degree that would disgrace a warrior of a savage tribe.*

—*Novanglus*, 1774–1775

Even in the heat of controversy over British treatment of the American colonies, John Adams took care to distinguish between "the [British] nation" and the man who created and administered most of Britain's policy regarding the colonies, prime minister and chancellor of the exchequer Frederick, Lord North. In this, Adams revealed his understanding that nations do not deal with nations, but that people deal with people.

**The Last Word:** All business is people business. Legally, contractually, one organization may have a relationship with another organization, but in any real-life, day-to-day sense, the relationship is between certain people in one organization and certain people in another. Every time you do business, keep it human. The higher the stakes, the greater the complexity, the more human it should be.

## Lesson 105
## THERE SLAVERY BEGINS

*And ... all ... elections ... should be annual, there not being in the whole circle of the sciences a maxim more infallible than this, "where annual elections end, there slavery begins."*

—"Thoughts on Government," 1776

A government, John Adams believed, needed "great men," but these were the very men he trusted least. Once a year, therefore, "these great men . . . should be, 'Like bubbles on the sea of matter borne,' [made to] 'rise . . . break, and to that sea return.'" Annual elections would "teach them the great political virtues of humility, patience, and moderation, without which every man in power becomes a ravenous beast of prey."

Historians have made much of the "political" differences between Thomas Jefferson and John Adams, identifying the former as the father of American government's Democratic-Republican strain, championing investment of power in the people, and the latter as that of the Federalist strain, favoring centralization of power. In fact, the major difference between these two founding fathers was less political than philosophical or even psychological. Whereas Jefferson believed in the essential goodness of humankind, its capacity for perfectibility, and the natural inevitability of the rise of the best of humanity to leadership of government, Adams saw the essential weakness of people, the inability of individuals to restrain the passions and appetites that, given the opportunity and the power, would transform them into "ravenous beast[s] of prey." Both men passionately fought for liberation, but Adams, just as passionately, advocated the apparatus of restraint to both manage and preserve that liberation.

*Revolutionary Wisdom*

"I dislike and detest hereditary honours, Offices Emoluments established by Law. So do you. I am for excluding legal hereditary distinctions from the U.S. as long as possible. So are you. I only say that Mankind have not yet discovered any remedy against irresistible Corruption in Elections to Offices of great Power and Profit, but making them hereditary."

—*Letter to Thomas Jefferson, November 15, 1813*

**The Last Word:** Any true leader understands that her position is not derived from a title—president, chairman, chief, boss, whatever—but is earned on an ongoing basis from those she leads. Annual elections? In business, the boss is elected every day, and when she stops winning those elections, her position becomes an empty title.

**Lesson 106**
## APPEAL TO YOUR ENEMY'S IMAGINATION

*. . . to show them the ruinous tendency of the war if continued another year or two. Where would England be if the war continued two years longer? What the state of her finances?*

—Diary, October 20, 1782

John Adams approached the negotiation of the treaty ending the American Revolution as an appeal to the imagination of the enemy. He asked the British treaty commissioners to imagine the consequences, to Britain, of continuing the war for a year or perhaps even two. He asked them to consider what would be the state of the nation's finances? Its "condition in the East and West Indies"? In Canada? In Ireland and Scotland? "What hopes," he asked, would the English people have of "saving themselves from a civil war?" Doubtless, the British commissioners came into the negotiation concerned about losing America. Adams maneuvered them into considering how much more would be lost if the hopeless war were continued.

**The Last Word:** The most powerful persuasion addresses neither the intellect nor the emotions alone, but engages the imagination, conjuring up a vision of reality either to be avoided or embraced.

**Lesson 107**

## MAKE DEFINITIONS PURE

*In the first place, what is your definition of a republic?*
—Letter to Roger Sherman, July 17, 1789

Everyone agrees that it is important to define the terms of an argument before launching into the argument. If the subject is fruit, and I think of apples but you of oranges, we will not get very far. In the worst case, our work will be destructive; at the best, it will be—well—fruitless.

In his epistolary debate with Roger Sherman on what structure of government should be embodied in the new Constitution, Adams cleared the air by defining his terms. He did so with the knowledge that the biggest, most consequential concepts are often not only the most vaguely defined, but defined in ways that carry a heavy emotional freight. Words like *republic, despotism,* and *monarchy* are all highly emotional, and, Adams believed, with the stakes so high—the very nature of a new government, for which Patriots sacrificed and died—it was absolutely necessary to state clear definitions divorced from connotation and the fog of mere emotion. Accordingly, he defined a republic with stark neutrality, as "*A government whose sovereignty is vested in more than one person.*" In contrast, a "despotism is a government in which the three divisions of power, the legislative, executive and judicial, are all vested in one man. A monarchy is a government where the legislative and executive are vested in one man, but the judicial in other men."

Not only did these definitions create clarity for the sake of rational, relatively unemotional argument, they revealed the nature of a republic in a new light, as a form of government in which sovereignty "might be vested in two persons, or in three millions, or in any other intermediate number." Moreover, a republic might well have strong elements of either a monarchy, a despotism, or an aristocracy, which Adams defined as a government in which sovereignty was entirely invested in a few men of certain distinction, whether of birth, property, intellect, or some combination of these. Adams's point was that there was nothing mystically or magically exclusive about the nature of a republic. Depending on how it was structured, it could embody the very vices and virtues of the kinds of governments it was meant to replace.

**The Last Word:** A good definition dispels not only the fog of emotion, but disposes of all mystification, thereby providing a clean and level platform for "amiable" argument.

## Lesson 108
### The Inevitability of Aristocracy

*By an aristocrat, I mean every man who can command or influence TWO VOTES; ONE BESIDES HIS OWN.*

—Letter to John Taylor, April 15, 1814

*Aristocracy* was one of those words and concepts so emotionally loaded that Adams felt the need of clearing the air with a careful definition of his own. Writing to his critic John Taylor, he came at it this way. He began by pointing out that, to the Greeks, "'aristocracy' originally signified 'the government of the best men.'" Now, Thomas Jefferson believed that the "best men"—what Jefferson called the "natural aristocrats"—would, in any free society, naturally and inevitably rise to positions of power and influence.

Adams disagreed. The best would not naturally—or even supernaturally—rise. Other men would judge of who was best. "But," Adams asked Taylor, "who are to be judges of the best men?" That was "the rub!" While it is true, Adams admitted, that despots, monarchs, and aristocrats—as well as democrats—"have, in all ages hit, at times, upon the best men. . . . But, at other times, and much more frequently, they have all chosen the very worst men; the men who have the most devotedly and the most slavishly flattered their vanity, gratified their most extravagant passions, and promoted their selfish and private views." This being the case, Adams turned from defining aristocrat as the "best" person or even as the person someone at sometime and in some place thought the "best" person to simply the most influential person: the person "who can command or influence TWO VOTES; ONE BESIDES HIS OWN."

What, Adams asked, are the consequences of this definition?

He invited Taylor to take "the first hundred men you meet" anywhere "and constitute them a democratical republic." Here is what will happen:

> When your new democratical republic meets, you will find half a dozen men of independent fortunes; half a dozen, of more eloquence; half a dozen, with more learning; half a dozen, with eloquence, learning, and fortune.
>
> Let me see. We have now four-and-twenty; to these we may add six more, who will have more art, cunning, and intrigue, than learning, eloquence, or fortune. These will infallibly soon unite with the twenty-four. Thus we make thirty. The remaining seventy are composed of farmers, shopkeepers, merchants, tradesmen, and laborers. Now, if each of these thirty can, by any means, influence one vote besides his own, the whole thirty can carry sixty votes,—a decided and uncontrolled majority of the hundred. These thirty I mean by aristocrats; and they will instantly convert your democracy of ONE HUNDRED into an aristocracy of THIRTY.

Democracy, Adams thus argued, inevitably becomes an aristocracy. There is neither good nor bad in this, but simply reality.

**The Last Word:** In any organization, influence becomes concentrated. Those charged with managing the organization must create mechanisms—in government, these are laws; in private enterprise, policies—to manage, first and foremost, the most influential, whoever they may prove to be at a particular moment in the history of the organization. Reliance on the so-called principle of democracy is not sufficient, since—whatever we may continue to call it—democracy will inevitably produce and then yield to aristocracy.

## Lesson 109
## THE FACT OF INEQUALITY

*Is there any thing in birth, however illustrious or splendid, which should make a difference between one man and another?*

—*Discourses on Davila*, 1790–1791

Among the "self-evident" truths Thomas Jefferson enumerated in the Declaration of Independence was the assertion that "all men are created equal." John Adams, who nominated Jefferson to write the Declaration in the first place, raised no objection to this statement, but he did not entirely endorse it, either. To be sure, he held that equality reigned absolute under law, but whereas many extreme democrats, Jefferson included, believed in a more universal equality among "men," Adams could not simply refute the proposition that "birth"—one's family origin—made a difference.

As was the case with Adams's thought generally, his position on distinction by birth—on the *inequality* among people—was fraught with well-pondered nuance. First, he attacked the notion: "If, from a common ancestor, the whole human race is descended, they are all of the same family. How then can they distinguish families into the more or less ancient? What advantage is there in an illustration of an hundred or a thousand years? Of what avail are all these histories, pedigrees, traditions?" Even if "birth" confers "some advantages of education," Adams conceded, such advantages "must be derived from his father and mother chiefly, if not wholly; of what importance is it then . . . whether the family is twenty generations upon record, or only two?"

For the likes of Jefferson, the question would be rhetorical. Birth is of no *real* consequence. But Adams pressed on, declaring that

"The mighty secret lies in this:—An illustrious descent attracts the notice of mankind."

It does not matter that birth confers no inherent distinction on a person. All that matters to Adams, whose focus is not on the individual but on the individual in society, is that birth creates the perception of distinction because it has the property of attracting notice. In itself, birth means nothing. In its effect, however, it is heavily freighted with significance, and although we might rightly and nobly declare all men to be created equal, they are not perceived as such. Whereas Jefferson and his followers would righteously endeavor to correct this erroneous perception, Adams accepted it as a social (if not biological) reality and sought to exploit it. "A good man," he wrote, "will neither be proud nor vain of his birth, but will earnestly improve every advantage he has for the public good." He will use the notice his birth attracts to create benefit for the nation.

**The Last Word:** In leading an enterprise, truth is a paramount value, but it is a mistake to reject out of hand the truth of perception in favor of the truth of principle. Perception, opinion, sentiment—all are facts in themselves. Sometimes it is necessary to change and correct them, and sometimes it is of more benefit to the enterprise to accept and to build on them. In no case can a manager simply ignore or reject them. To do so would be to deny reality.

## Lesson 110
## THE IMPOSSIBILITY OF PERFECT EQUALITY

*We are told that our friends, the National Assembly of France, have abolished all distinctions. Be not deceived, my dear countrymen. Impossibilities cannot be performed.*

—*Discourses on Davila*, 1790–1791

Adams believed in the absolute and natural equality of human rights. He also believed in reality, and the reality was that equality—except under the law—was an impossibility:

> Have they leveled all fortunes and equally divided all property? Have they made all men and women equally wise, elegant, and beautiful? Have they annihilated the names of Bourbon and Montmorenci, Rochefoucauld and Noailles, Lafayette and La Moignon, Necker and De Calonne, Mirabeau and Bailly? Have they committed to the flames all the records, annals, and histories of the nation? All the copies of Mezerai, Daniel, De Thou, Velly, and a thousand others? Have they burned all their pictures, and broken all their statues? Have they blotted out of all memories, the names, places of abode, and illustrious actions of all their ancestors? Have they not still princes of the first and second order, nobles and knights? Have they no record nor memory who are the men who compose the present national assembly? Do they wish to have that distinction forgotten? Have the French officers who served in America melted their eagles and torn their ribbons?

*Revolutionary Wisdom*
"In Truth my 'defence of the Constitutions' and 'Discourses on Davila,' laid the foundation of that immense Unpopularity, which fell like the Tower of Siloam upon me. Your steady defence of democratical Principles, and your invariable favourable Opinion of the French Revolution laid the foundation of your Unbounded Popularity. Sic transit Gloria Mundi."
—*Letter to Thomas Jefferson, July 13, 1813*

**The Last Word:** Everyone must be treated fairly and without prejudice. Yet, as every manager knows, some members of the organization are more experienced, more skillful, more creative, more cooperative than others. Some specialize in one area, while the expertise of others lies elsewhere. And, yes, some people—as productive contributors to the enterprise—are more valuable than others. This is a reality that must not be confused with the universal and absolute requirement that we respect—equally—the human value of everyone.

## Lesson 111
## Dictatorship by Committee

*The men of letters in France are wisely reforming one feudal system; but may they not, unwisely, lay the foundation of another?*

—*Discourses on Davila*, 1790–1791

In sharp contrast to Thomas Jefferson, John Adams was highly skeptical about the results of the French Revolution, even before the Reign of Terror gave everyone ample reason for skepticism and more. His concern was that by simply replacing the monarchy with a single assembly—what would become the Directory—the French were laying the foundation for a new feudal system. No longer would all power be invested in a single monarch, it is true, but it would be delivered nevertheless entirely to a single group. "A legislature, in one assembly," Adams argued, "can have no other termination than in civil dissension, feudal anarchy, or simple monarchy." In effect, a monolithic assembly, popularly elected, tends to divide into parties, whose purpose is to usurp all power and, in so doing, replace representative government with a collective dictatorship. Power, Adams understood, is a fact, necessary to any government. Unchecked, power—absolute power—is also inimical to government. Yet merely transferring power from one person to several—dozens, hundreds, or even thousands—in an assembly does not provide the necessary check. All power must be balanced by power. For this reason, Adams advocated a bicameral legislature, consisting of a popularly elected lower house and an appointed upper house, each of which would serve as a check and balance on the other.

*Revolutionary Wisdom*

"The best apology which can be made for . . . sovereignty in one assembly . . . is that it is only intended to be momentary. If a senate had been proposed [as a second assembly in post-revolutionary France], it must have been formed, most probably, of princes of the blood, cardinals, archibishops, dukes, and marquises; and all these together would have obstructed the progress of the reformation in religion and government, and procured an abortion to the regeneration of France. Pennsylvania established her single assembly, in 1776, upon the same principle. An apprehension, that the Proprietary and Quaker interests would prevail, to the election of characters disaffected to the American cause, finally preponderated against two legislative councils. Pennsylvania, and Georgia, who followed her example, have found by experience the necessity of change; and France, by the same infallible progress of reasoning, will discover the same necessity; happy, indeed, if the experiment shall not cost her more dear."

—*Discourses on Davila, 1790–1791*

**The Last Word:** Leading any complex enterprise requires delegating and even sharing authority. But a committee can rule as arbitrarily and as unwisely as a single boss. In delegating authority, it is always dangerous merely to pass the buck. A mechanism of review, oversight, and revision is an essential aspect of management.

**Lesson 112**
## THE GREAT ART OF LAWGIVING

*The essence of a free government consists in an effectual control of rivalries.*
—*Discourses on Davila*, 1790–1791

No population is uniform in its needs and desires. No population is uniformly rich or poor. No population is without rivalries. To deny these facts is to make the creation of an effective free government impossible. Adams did not believe that a free government could bring absolute unity, but that it could—and must—control rivalries, which are inevitable, endemic, and real. The error of the French Revolution, Adams believed, was its effort to eliminate rivalry by leveling wealth. To give any individual or group "unlimited or unbalanced power of disposing property"—especially giving the power to "those who have no property"—is to commit "the lamb . . . to the custody of the wolf."

For Adams, government could not be about eliminating disparities in wealth, leveling differences, and extinguishing rivalries, but about "balancing the poor against the rich in the legislature, and in constituting the legislative a perfect balance against the executive power, at the same time that no individual or party can become its rival." Failing this, the "nation which will not adopt an equilibrium of power must adopt a despotism. There is no other alternative."

*Revolutionary Wisdom*
"The judicial power ought to be distinct from both the legislative and the executive, and independent upon both, that

so it may be a check upon both, as both should be checks
upon that."

— *"Thoughts on Government,"* 1776

**The Last Word:** Management cannot emulate Genesis, creating something from nothing. Management is always confronted with something, a reality that includes people and departments and functions with different needs, problems, and wants, some of which inevitably conflict. Such needs, problems, wants, and conflicts cannot be eliminated or ignored. They can—and must—be balanced through policies, mechanisms, and management attitudes that account for everything and everyone in some productive way. Reality cannot be legislated out of existence. It must be accommodated as well as controlled and profitably exploited.

## Lesson 113
## Can't Fix People

*[R]emember that the perfectibility of man is only human and terrestrial perfectibility.*

—*Discourses on Davila*, 1790–1791

Thomas Jefferson's theory of government rested on what he believed was the essential goodness of human beings, a natural desire, as it were, for good and beneficent government—a desire that might be perverted and deformed and denied by tyrants, but that nevertheless existed and, given the opportunity, would manifest itself. John Adams saw this as a belief in the "perfectibility" of man, and while he was willing to believe that people could improve themselves, they were limited by the reality of life itself. Human perfectibility was of necessity "terrestrial," not divine, and, on earth, reality was reality: "Cold will still freeze, and fire will never cease to burn; disease and vice will continue to disorder, and death to terrify mankind. Emulation next to self-preservation will forever be the great spring of human actions, and the balance of well-ordered government will alone be able to prevent that emulation from degenerating into dangerous ambition, irregular rivalries, destructive factions, wasting seditions, and bloody, civil wars."

*Revolutionary Wisdom*

"You was well persuaded in your own mind that the Nation would succeed in establishing a free Republican Government: I was as well persuaded, in mine, that a project of such a Government, over five and twenty millions people, when four and twenty millions and five hundred thousands of them could

neither write nor read: was as unnatural irrational and imprac-
ticable; as it would be over the Elephants Lions Tigers Panthers
Wolves and Bears in the Royal Menagerie, at Versailles."
                                    —*Letter to Thomas Jefferson, July 13, 1813*

**The Last Word:** The point for rational leadership and sound
management is not to avoid expecting too much of people. You
should, in fact, expect great things. Set the bar high, even higher
than you think reasonable or realistic. But you should understand
that it is, quite simply, crazy to attempt to fix people. You can
educate, correct, and encourage, but you cannot create essential
change. For that reason, focus on issues rather than personalities.
Policies, procedures, and products are far more perfectible than
people.

**Lesson 114**

## CHANGE HAPPENS (BUT RELATIVE STABILITY IS POSSIBLE)

*[I]n one sense, nothing in human affairs will be perpetual or at rest, [but] the duration of our lives, the security of our property, the existence of our conveniences, comforts, and pleasures, the repose of private life, and the tranquility of society, are placed in very great degrees of human power.*

—*Discourses on Davila*, 1790–1791

"The best," runs an old saying, "is the enemy of the good." In seeking perfection and bewailing the impossibility of achieving it, we may fail to exploit opportunities for creating any number of benefits that are very good, albeit imperfect. The leader of any business who seeks permanence fails to accept the reality of business—or any system of transaction—which is change. Indeed, Adams recognized that life itself is change, a "chemical process . . . carried on by unceasing motion." All matter was, for him, subject to "mutability and mutations" as a "consequence of the laws of nature." To single-mindedly seek permanence is to find only frustration and, even worse, to fail to achieve the degree of stability that is possible and that, in civilized life, yields longevity, security, comfort, convenience, and tranquility—albeit in relative rather than absolute degrees.

**The Last Word:** All organized endeavors are mutable and impermanent. Theoretically, stability is impossible. Practically, however, it is the very essence of management, which seeks to create endurance and durability within the relentlessly dynamic universe of commerce.

**Lesson 115**

## THE LIMIT OF EQUALITY

*[T]he golden rule; do as you would be done by; is all the Equality that can be supported or defended by reason, or reconciled to common Sense.*
                    —Letter to Thomas Jefferson, July 13, 1813

"I have never read Reasoning more absurd, Sophistry more gross . . . than the subtle labours of [the Enlightenment philosophers Claude Adrien] Helvetius and [Jean-Jacques] Rousseau to demonstrate the natural Equality of Mankind." In this assessment, John Adams bucked the trend of the Romantic revolutionary thinking that thoroughly captivated the likes of Thomas Jefferson. Indeed, it was for such declarations that Adams drew charges of being a reactionary and a "monarchist." Yet the fact was that John Adams had been a revolutionary and remained a believer and champion of free government. What he refused to do is toe the party line of most others who called themselves revolutionaries, republicans, or democrats. Equal justice under the law did not require subscribing to a doctrine of absolute equality in all physical, intellectual, spiritual, and emotional attributes. The limit of equality compatible with the reality of human diversity was 100 percent moral. It was the application of the golden rule, the treatment of others as you yourself would want to be treated. For all leaders and managers, this remains the most viable standard of fair treatment.

*Revolutionary Wisdom*
"Let me now ask you, very seriously my Friend, Where are now in 1813, the Perfection and perfectability of human Nature? Where is now, the progress of the human Mind?

Where is the Amelioration of Society? Where the Augmentations of human Comforts? Where the diminutions of human Pains and Miseries? . . . When? Where? And how? is the present Chaos to be arranged into Order?"

—*Letter to Thomas Jefferson, July 15, 1813*

**The Last Word:** There would be no reason for businesses bigger than a mom-and-pop shop or even a single-owner operation if most of the jobs civilization required doing did not call for a diversity of competences, of knowledge, of talents, of interests, of points of view. Inequality is the very basis of any serious organized endeavor, but it does not preclude justice, decency, and respect. Indeed, the diversity of any complex organization demands justice, decency, and respect, without which the enterprise becomes a mob.

**Lesson 116**

## HOW LEVEL CAN A FIELD BE?

*When the two are reduced to beggars, will they have as much influence in society as any one of the four?*

—Letter to John Taylor, April 15, 1814

Were society's playing field miraculously made level by an equitable redistribution of wealth, what would happen?

Adams posed a hypothetical case to his philosophical adversary and critic John Taylor. Assume a family of six sons, he wrote, four of whom are "prudent, discreet, frugal and industrious," the other two "idle and profligate." The father leaves each son an equal portion of his estate. "How long will it be before the two will request the four to purchase their shares? and how long before the purchase money will be spent in sports, gambled away at a race, or cards, or dice, or billiards, or dissipated at taverns or worse houses? When the two are reduced to beggars, will they have as much influence in society as any one of the four?"

**The Last Word:** Equality in society or any group is nearly impossible to establish and absolutely impossible to perpetuate. This is a reality both of national government and entrepreneurial management. It is neither wrong nor right, deplorable nor desirable. It is real.

**Lesson 117**

## Equal Rights Without Equal Power

*They have all equal rights; but cannot, and ought not to have equal power.*
—Letter to John Taylor, April 15, 1814

In a letter to John Taylor, who had published a book critical of Adams's political philosophy, Adams invited his correspondent to imagine a family of six daughters, four "not only beautiful, but serious and discreet," two "not only ugly, but ill tempered and immodest." Who among these six, he asked, will have the greatest chance of attracting a "husband of worth, respectability, and consideration in the world?" The obvious answer, Adams believed, instantly demonstrated that the "imagination . . . of a government, of a democratical republic, in which every man and every woman shall have an equal weight in society, is a chimera," an illusion.

John Adams refused to build a system of government on an illusion. Inequality is reality in all aspects of life in society—life within an organization—except where the law is concerned. Yet while everyone is equal under the law, different people enjoy varying degrees of power and influence according to their perceived value to the members of the society or organization.

**The Last Word:** All leaders, every manager, must be fair, but they must also recognize the value of influence and of influential people. It is through them that you are enabled to move, shape, and motivate the entire enterprise.

**Lesson 118**
ABSOLUTE POWER, ABSOLUTE INTOXICATION

*[A]bsolute power intoxicates alike despots, monarchs, aristocrats, and democrats, and Jacobins, and sans culottes. I cannot say that democracy has been more pernicious, on the whole, than any of the others.*
—Letter to John Taylor, April 15, 1814

No form of government changes the nature of absolute power, a force that intoxicates everyone of every political and philosophical stripe. Democracy is no safeguard against this intoxication, and is no more effective at regulating power than it is at controlling any other human weakness, scourge, or passion.

John Adams believed in free government, but he did not deceive himself into thinking that democracy was a panacea in the management of power. Regardless of the philosophy behind any government, only a system in which one power was enabled to check another power (and that power to be checked in its turn) could reliably prevent power from becoming absolute in the hands of any one individual or set of individuals.

**The Last Word:** Do not seduce yourself or others with words, slogans, and formulas. Understand the underlying principles in any system and the driving values in any organization. Manage these for what they really are, regardless of what they may be called.

**Lesson 119**

## OF LIBERTY

*[Liberty] is a self-determining power in an intellectual agent. It implies thought and choice and power; it can elect between objects, indifferent in point of morality, neither morally good nor morally evil.*
—Letter to John Taylor, April 15, 1814

Liberty, the very concept at the heart of the American Revolution and the rock upon which American government was founded, was, Adams realized, a concept imperfectly understood. Most advocates of liberty saw it as a moral force, in effect the embodiment of good in government versus evil in government. Adams, however, regarded liberty as a morally neutral "attribute," nothing more or less than "a self-determining power in an intellectual agent," the unfettered faculty of thought, choice, and power capable of electing between objects, without necessary regard to their relative morality. In short, liberty was choice in its purest possible form, uncoerced (as by some tyrant), but also not necessarily informed (as by some principles of morality). For Adams, liberty resembled any other power in that it was raw, as freedom of will is raw—essential in a free society, to be sure, but neither good nor bad in itself and certainly not guaranteed to make laudable, desirable, or constructive choices.

**The Last Word:** Liberty is a tool, capable of being used or abused, used with skill or used clumsily, used to build up or used to tear down. The leader who can give the gift of liberty to his followers is a great leader—but only up to the point that, having bestowed liberty, he turns his back and simply allows the people to do with it as they will. Then he stops being a leader, great or otherwise. Liberty is a management means, not an end.

# Chapter 8

# Legacy

## Lesson 120
### The Commonwealth of Paradise

*Suppose a nation in some distant region should take the Bible for their only law-book, and every member should regulate his conduct by the precepts there exhibited!*

—Diary, February 22, 1756

Young John Adams mused in his diary about a utopian society that took only the Bible for its law book. The result, as he saw it, would not be an Old Testament world of fundamentalism ruled by an angry God, but a "commonwealth" in which "no man would impair his health by gluttony, drunkenness, or lust." There would be no theft, no gambling, no lying, no fraud, but all would "live in peace and good will with all men" and worship with a "rational and manly, a sincere and unaffected piety." Such a commonwealth, Adams thought, would be "a Paradise."

For John Adams, neither temporal law nor the Bible was a set of societal rules. Rather, both were shapers of individual character. Ideally, laws were not established to set social standards, but to build individual character—that is, build society one person at a time. Only if law were thoroughly inculcated at this individual level, as a kind of religion, would society become utopian, a paradise, in the fullest sense a commonwealth.

*Revolutionary Wisdom*
"All day in high health and spirits. That comet which appeared in 1682 is expected again this year; and we have intelligence that it has been seen about ten days since, near midnight, in the east. I find myself very much inclined to an unreasonable absence of mind, and to a morose and unsociable disposition; let it therefore be my constant endeavor to reform these great faults."

—*Diary, February 24, 1756*

**The Last Word:** Shaping an enterprise is not a matter of imposing rules on the organization, but persuading each who participates to invest in its values individually and deeply. Any enterprise, whether it is a national body politic, a vast corporation, or a small business, is most enduringly and effectively constructed from the inside out, beginning on the level of the individual rather than on that of the organization. For this reason, an effective manager must be a leader, a coach, and even something of a preacher.

**Lesson 121**

## TO LEARN, IMBIBE

*We are told that Demosthenes transcribed the history of Thucydides eight times, in order to imbibe and familiarize himself with the elegance and strength of his style.*

—Diary, February 24, 1756

John Adams did not merely study a subject, he imbibed it, drank it in. This was especially true of the law, which, as he saw it, was nothing less than a system for the productive regulation of civilized life.

He noted with pleasure that he was not alone in the intensity of his study. The Greek orator Demosthenes (384–322 B.C.), Adams discovered, had not merely read Thucydides—known as the father of history—but had read and transcribed his massive body of work no fewer than eight times so that he might "imbibe" the qualities of the great writer's style.

**The Last Word:** Learn from the best. Just don't expect exceptional results from casual study. Immerse yourself in your model. Imbibe his or her work.

**Lesson 122**

## THE AMERICAN EXAMPLE

*It was this great struggle that peopled America.*
—*A Dissertation on the Canon and Feudal Law,* 1765

In John Adams's view of history, the Great Reformation that began in the sixteenth century was essentially a rebirth and dissemination of knowledge after a long period of enforced ignorance under canon and feudal law. In proportion as knowledge "increased and spread among the people," Adams wrote, "ecclesiastical and civil tyranny, which I use as synonymous expressions for the canon and feudal laws, seems to have lost their strength and weight. The people grew more and more sensible of the wrong that was done them by these systems, more and more impatient under it, and determined at all hazards to rid themselves of it." One result was the English Civil War, which toppled what Adams called the "confederacy . . . of temporal and spiritual tyranny," a conspiracy of church and state. Another result was the peopling of America. "It was not religion alone, as is commonly supposed," Adams wrote, "but it was love of universal liberty . . . that projected, conducted, and accomplished the settlement of America."

As early as 1765, when the colonies became united in opposition to that aspect of English tyranny known as the Stamp Act, Adams was at pains to bring evidence showing that the desire for liberty was no novel invention of American malcontents, but a product of history. It was part and parcel of the Puritan heritage of America. It was also a movement that laid claim to nothing new, but, rather, to ancient rights of English men and women, guaranteed by the Magna Carta of 1215. Yet Adams was also at pains to show that the

Puritans did not undertake their action lightly, however justified it was. Theirs "was a resolution formed by a sensible people," Adams wrote, "almost in despair." It was the last resort of those who had "much reason to despair of deliverance from" the religious persecution that characterized life under government "on that side of the ocean."

No sooner did the Puritans arrive in America than they "formed their plan, both of ecclesiastical and civil government, in direct opposition to the canon and feudal systems." But they did not simply tear down an old system. Their "leading men," Adams pointed out, "were men of sense and learning." They were familiar with the thinkers of Greece and Rome, and they used their ancient example as a pattern for constructing a new society.

Paradox is at the heart of John Adams's philosophy of government. A revolutionary, he set his eyes on the future, yet always built upon the past. His concept of revolution was not as the most radical political step a people can take, but as the most conservative—a means of securing, recovering, repossessing ancient (even timeless) rights that had, through tyranny, been denied. For Adams, the future was a return to ancient Greece and Rome or to the era of the Magna Carta or to the arrival of the Puritans in New England. The future was largely made of the past.

*Revolutionary Wisdom*

"The Parson [Lemuel Bryant, the "parish priest" of John Adams's boyhood] and the Pedagogue [Joseph Cleverly, "my Latin School Master"] lived much together, but were eternally disputing about Government and Religion. One day, when the Schoolmaster had been more than commonly fanatical, and declared 'if he were a Monark, *He would have but one Religion in his Dominions'* The Parson coolly replied 'Cleverly! You would be the best Man in the World, if You had no Religion.'"

—*Letter to Thomas Jefferson, April 19, 1817*

**The Last Word:** Innovation, change, "new blood" are typically regarded as unquestionably good for any dynamic endeavor. And it is true: the enterprise that fails to adapt to developing challenges as well as to shape new opportunities is doomed. Yet this does not require the wholesale repudiation of history. Development, evolution, even revolution can be productively reared on what has gone before. Managing successful change calls for an ability to tell the difference between fluid particulars and solid principles as well as for the skill and discipline to transform the former without abandoning, compromising, or destroying the latter.

## Lesson 123
EDUCATION

---

*[E]ducation . . . no expense for this purpose would be thought too extravagant.*

—"Thoughts on Government," 1776

No American political leader has ever come out publicly against education, and most have at least voiced enthusiastic support for it. Yet what governor or president in American history ever proclaimed, as John Adams did in 1776, that "Laws for the liberal education of youth, especially of the lower class of people, are so extremely wise and useful, that, to a humane and generous mind, no expense for this purpose would be thought too extravagant"?

The question, unfortunately, is rhetorical. With the exception of Thomas Jefferson—who created a university—no national leader since Adams has so deeply believed in education as the essence of democracy. A state of nature, Adams believed, was by definition a state of ignorance, and to entrust governing power to ignorance was folly. The more ignorant a people, the more they are likely to abuse, misuse, or simply lose political power and, with it, their liberty. In a state of ignorance, fear quickly replaces prudent judgment. Knowledge is incompatible both with fear and with tyranny. Educate the people, and you increase the chances of successful democratic government.

Most modern enterprises recognize the importance of creating an educated workforce; few, however, extend educational support beyond training that is directly related to a particular job. Adams advocated a *liberal* education, education of the whole person, rather than simply training for a particular function.

*Revolutionary Wisdom*

"Education! Oh Education! The greatest Grief of my heart, and the greatest Affliction of my Life! To my mortification I must confess, that I have never closely thought, or very deliberately reflected upon the Subject, which never occurs to me now, without producing a deep Sigh, an heavy groan and sometimes Tears. My cruel Destiny separated me from my Children, allmost continually from their Birth to their Manhood. I was compelled to leave them to the ordinary routine of reading writing and Latin School, Academy and Colledge. . . . If I venture to give you any thoughts at all, they must be very crude."

*—Response, in a letter to Thomas Jefferson, July 16, 1814, to Jefferson's request for Adams's detailed thoughts on education*

**The Last Word:** Managers require personnel skilled in a variety of functions, but the enduring success of an organization also depends on employees who understand more than their jobs. It depends on people capable of understanding the entire nature of the enterprise and its role in the marketplace and the community, and capable as well of reinventing those roles as the future may require. The intelligence of an organization is—no surprise here—a product of the intelligence of its members.

## Lesson 124
## LETTING IT BE

*I have well fixed it in my Mind as a Principle, that every Nation has a Right to that Religion and Government, which it chooses, and as long as any People please themselves in these great Points, I am determined they shall not displease me.*

—Letter to Abigail Adams, June 3, 1778

John Adams was delighted by the French countryside outside of Paris, writing to his wife that the country was "one great Garden," in which "Nature and Art have conspired to render every Thing . . . delightful." In telling Abigail this, he anticipated her objection. Delightful? "Religion and Government, you will say ought to be excepted." True, he admitted, these were objectionable in France, but they were "no Afflictions to me." He told Abigail Adams that he had decided that each nation had the right to choose to live and govern itself as it wished. For his part, John Adams would let it be.

Adams's willingness to tolerate morals and systems of government of whatever sort in countries not his own ran contrary to such philosophers of revolution as Thomas Paine and Thomas Jefferson. For them, the American Revolution and, with it, the ideals of democracy and republicanism were aspects of a world movement, a movement rightly encompassing all of humankind. It is this view that would often influence, for better or worse, American foreign policy, including William McKinley's decision to go to war with Spain over Cuban independence in 1898, Woodrow Wilson's decision to bring the United States into World War I, the essence of Franklin Roosevelt's policies in World War II, America's conduct throughout the era of the Cold War, and, most recently, the decision to invade Iraq for the purpose of "bringing democracy" to that nation.

**The Last Word:** The decision of whether to act to shape the environment beyond one's own enterprise is not restricted to the leaders of nations. Corporate leaders often act to influence public opinion as well as public policy through initiatives ranging from public relations campaigns to lobbying and other political campaigns. Adams was wary of any venture beyond his own government and advocated a philosophy of live and let live. In the twentieth century, this might have been criticized as isolationist. Perhaps. But at the very least, the example of John Adams should serve as a check and balance on corporate ambition and the desire to remake all the world in one's own image.

## Lesson 125
### Free and Amicable Intercourse

---

*It is by a free and amicable intercourse of sentiments, that the friends of our country may hope for such a unanimity of opinion and such a concert of exertions, as may sooner or later produce the blessings of good government.*

—Letter to Roger Sherman, July 17, 1789

Roger Sherman of Connecticut, one of the architects of the Constitution, believed in the decentralization of power, with sovereignty lodged chiefly in the legislative branch. Adams, in contrast, sought for centralization, with sovereignty to be divided between a legislative and executive branch, while an independent judicial branch held certain powers overruling either of the other two branches within the compass of the law. Ignoring the main thrust of Adams's position, which was a system of checks and balances, Sherman and others accused him of simply favoring the executive branch, which, they claimed, was really a disguised form of monarchy.

John Adams was a man of quick temper, but when it came to hammering out the structure of American government, he held personal passion in check and was determined to refrain from attacking personalities and to avoid as well taking attacks on his position personally. Instead, he opened up a lively debate with his chief ideological opponents, a debate memorialized in a remarkable exchange of correspondence. His object was to maintain the focus on issues, which, he knew, would endure far longer than the individuals behind them. To maintain this focus, he urged an "amicable" debate not aimed at the goal of creating a winner and a loser, but of producing "the blessings of good government . . . sooner or later."

*Revolutionary Wisdom*

"A pen is certainly an excellent instrument to fix a man's attention and to enflame his ambition."

*Diary, November 14, 1760*

**The Last Word:** Disagreement, dispute, and debate are vital to managing a great enterprise—provided that they do not degenerate into a battle of individual wills, egos, and personalities. People are important, but they do not last as long as important ideas and valued principles. The good stewardship of any organization requires all advocates of opposing positions to be, first and last and above all, "friends" of the enterprise. Whatever else they may disagree about, all members of the enterprise need to have the good of the enterprise in common.

## Lesson 126
## AT A STAND

*While all other Sciences have advanced, that of Government is at a stand;
little better understood; little better practiced now than 3 or 4 thousand
Years ago.*

—Letter to Thomas Jefferson, July 9, 1813

Government, the management of human affairs in society, had
failed to progress, Adams wrote to Jefferson, since the age of the
Greeks and Romans. The reason is that "Parties and Factions will
not suffer, or permit Improvements to be made," and rivalry, a basic
human passion, likewise interferes. "As soon as one Man hints at an
improvement his Rival opposes it. No sooner has one Party discovered or invented an Amelioration of the Condition of Man or the
order of Society, than the opposite Party, belies it, misconstrues it,
misrepresents it, ridicules it, insults it, and persecutes it."

And it gets worse. "Records are destroyed. Histories are annihi-
lated or interpolated, or prohibited sometimes by Popes, sometimes
by Emperors, sometimes by Aristocratical and sometimes by democratical Assemblies and sometimes by Mobs."

There is, Adams believed, a basic, natural drive that compels
us to focus on ourselves at the expense of the group. This in itself is
hardly unnatural; survival, after all, is a perfectly rational and reasonable goal. But the irony is that, in organized, civilized society, such
self-centeredness is ultimately *self*-destructive—destructive of the
individual. If the government fails, if the nation fails, if the society
fails, if the enterprise fails, the individual is put into peril. Adams
saw the great paradox of government—the management of human
affairs in society—as the necessity to prompt, to persuade, to cajole,
and sometimes to coerce people to think and act counterintuitively.

For the good of the organization, they had to be made to think and act beyond themselves, sometimes even against their own apparent, or at least immediate, self-interest. Sacrifice and duty had to be made to figure as importantly for each individual as self-fulfillment and self-gratification do. The leader's task is, therefore, to advance the science of government by creating systems that not only elicit self-sacrifice, but do so on a basis that continually demonstrates the connection between that sacrifice and survival. The alternative, as Adams saw it, is an individual power grab leading to anarchy.

**The Last Word:** Within the context of any commonwealth—an enterprise organized for the common benefit—egocentric thought and behavior are fatal. They are, in fact, a case of murder-suicide, killing the commonwealth, which also kills the individual. The means of preventing this—Adams called it government; we may call it management—seemed to Adams to be in urgent need of fresh study, having been largely neglected since about 3000 B.C.

**Lesson 127**

## USE WHAT WORKS

*Be to their faults a little blind; to their Virtues ever kind.*
—Letter to Thomas Jefferson, July 16, 1813

"All a little cracked!" That is how John Adams described to his friend and adversary Thomas Jefferson the following people: Plato, Rousseau, Paine, Bollingbroke, Hume, Gibbon, Voltaire, Turgot, Helvetius, Diderot, Condorcet, Buffon, de la Lande, "and fifty others," some of the most influential thinkers, scientists, and philosophers of Western civilization.

"All a little cracked!" And it did not matter, at least not much. Flawed as they were, each in their way, Adams counseled accepting them for what they had to offer instead of rejecting them for their flaws.

**The Last Word:** Adams never scorned the good for failing to be great, the useful for not being perfect. This did not mean that he accepted everything and everyone uncritically, but he took them for what they might contribute rather than condemned them for failing to contribute absolutely everything. After all, if perfection were possible, government—or management of any kind—would be superfluous.

**Lesson 128**

## MODELS FOR MANAGEMENT

*Study government as you build ships or construct steam-engines.*
—Letter to John Taylor, April 15, 1814

"The steam frigate will not defend New York," Adams wrote, "if Nature has not been studied, and her principles regarded. And how is the nature of man, and of society, and of government, to be studied or known, but in the history and by the experience of human nature in its terrestrial existence?"

Shakespeare's King Lear raves, "[n]othing will come of nothing," and although the sentiment comes from his madness, it is true nevertheless. Management is a daunting task. If, however, you believe that it requires the creation of systems of "government" out of nothing but your own brain, you transform a daunting task into an impossible one.

**The Last Word:** Every organization that has ever been— whether a nation or a shoe store—has been managed, poorly or well, but managed nonetheless. Models of management therefore abound. They are there to be studied, not in any slavish or passive way, but critically, evaluating the effects and results of each system. Build yours on the best of these. And while you are not obliged to remake whatever systems you may have inherited from predecessors, consider doing so anyway, albeit in the light of "history and . . . human nature."

# A John Adams Timeline

**1735**
OCTOBER 30: Born in Braintree (modern Quincy), Massachusetts

**1751–1755**
Attends Harvard College, graduates July 1755

**1755**
AUGUST: Begins teaching in Worcester, Massachusetts

**1756**
AUGUST: Begins law studies with James Putnam, Worcester

**1758**
NOVEMBER: Admitted to the bar, Suffolk County, Massachusetts

**1763**
JUNE–JULY: Publishes first newspaper writings

**1764**
OCTOBER 25: Marries Abigail Smith, Weymouth, Massachusetts

**1765**
JULY 14: Daughter Abigail (Nabby) born
AUGUST–OCTOBER: Publishes *Dissertation on the Canon and Feudal Law*
SEPTEMBER: Publishes "Instructions of the Town of Braintree to Their Representative," a denunciation of the Stamp Act

**1767**
JULY 11: Son John Quincy Adams born

**1768**
DECEMBER 28: Daughter Susanna Adams born

## 1770

**January:** Becomes clerk, Suffolk County Bar Association
**February 4:** Infant daughter Susanna Adams dies
**May 29:** Son Charles Adams born
**June:** Elected Boston representative to the General Court
**October–November:** Defends British soldiers in the Boston Massacre trials

## 1772

**September 15:** Son Thomas Boylston Adams born

## 1774

**September–October:** Delegate to first Continental Congress, Philadelphia
**December:** Begins publication of *Novanglus* essays

## 1775

**April:** Last of *Novanglus* essays published
**May–July and September–December:** Attends second Continental Congress.
**June 15:** Nominates George Washington as commander in chief, Continental Army
**June 17:** Witnesses Battle of Bunker Hill
**July:** Elected to the Massachusetts Council
**October 28:** Appointed chief justice of Massachusetts (does not serve, resigning on February 10, 1777)

## 1776

**February–October:** Continues service in the Continental Congress
**March–April:** Composes *Thoughts on Government*
**June 13:** Named president of the Board of War
**June–July:** Serves on the Declaration of Independence committee
**June–September:** Drafts "Plan of Treaties," the nation's first outline of foreign policy

## 1777
January–November: Continues service in the Continental Congress
July 11: Daughter Elizabeth Adams stillborn
November 27: Elected (by Congress) commissioner to France (with Benjamin Franklin and Arthur Lee)

## 1778
February 14–April 1: Sails with John Quincy Adams to France
May 8: First audience with Louis XVI

## 1779
June 17–August 3: Returns to Boston
August: Proposes founding the American Academy of Arts and Sciences (established 1780)
September–October: Drafts the Massachusetts Constitution of 1780 (adopted October 25, 1780)
September 27: Named to negotiate treaties of peace and commerce with Great Britain
November 15–February 9, 1780: Journeys (with John Quincy and Charles Adams) by sea and overland to Paris for peace negotiation

## 1780
June: Commissioned by Congress to negotiate a loan from the Dutch republic
July: Writes "Letters from a Distinguished American"
July 27–August 10: Travels (with John Quincy and Charles Adams) to Amsterdam
October 4–27: Writes a series of letters to one Hendrik Calkoen to explain the American Revolution to the Dutch people
December 29: Commissioned by Congress to negotiate a commercial treaty with the Dutch republic

## 1781

**APRIL 19:** Dutch republic recognizes United States independence
**APRIL 22:** Adams appointed minister plenipotentiary (effectively ambassador) to the Dutch republic
**MAY 12:** Establishes the first U.S. embassy, at the Hague
**JUNE 11:** Obtains Dutch loan
**JUNE 15:** Revoking Adams's commissions to negotiate treaties with the British, Congress appoints Adams to a joint commission, with Benjamin Franklin, John Jay, Henry Laurens, and Thomas Jefferson
**AUGUST–OCTOBER:** Bout of illness in Amsterdam
**OCTOBER 8:** Concludes treaty of amity and commerce with the Dutch republic
**NOVEMBER 30:** With Benjamin Franklin and John Jay, signs a preliminary peace treaty with Great Britain

## 1783

**SEPTEMBER 3:** Signs the final peace treaty with Great Britain

## 1784

**MARCH 9:** Obtains second Dutch loan
**MAY–JUNE:** Elected (with Benjamin Franklin and Thomas Jefferson) commissioner to negotiate treaties of amity and commerce with European and North African nations

## 1785

**FEBRUARY 24:** Appointed first U.S. minister (effectively ambassador) to Great Britain
**JULY 2:** Establishes first American legation in London
**AUGUST 5:** Signs a treaty of amity and commerce with Prussia

## 1786

**JANUARY 25:** Signs a treaty of peace and friendship with Morocco
**MARCH–APRIL:** With Thomas Jefferson, negotiates commercial treaties with Tripoli, Portugal, and Great Britain
**SEPTEMBER–OCTOBER:** Begins writing *A Defence of the Constitutions of the United States* (completed 1787)

**1787**

MAY–JUNE: Negotiates third Dutch loan

**1788**

FEBRUARY–MARCH: Negotiates fourth Dutch loan

APRIL–JUNE: Returns to Massachusetts

**1789**

MARCH: Elected the first vice president of the United States

**1790**

APRIL: Begins serial publication of *Discourses on Davila* (concludes April 1791)

NOVEMBER: John and Abigail Adams move to the new capital city, Philadelphia

**1791**

MAY: Elected president of the Academy of Arts and Sciences (serves until 1813)

**1793**

FEBRUARY: Reelected vice president of the United States

**1795**

JANUARY 27 OR 28: Caroline Amelia Smith, daughter of Abigail Adams Smith, born in New York

AUGUST 29: Charles Adams marries Sarah Smith, sister of William Stephens Smith, in New York

**1796**

DECEMBER: Elected second president of the United States, narrowly defeating Thomas Jefferson, who (under the law at the time) becomes vice president

**1797**

MARCH 4: Inaugurated

JUNE 1: Appoints John Quincy Adams minister plenipotentiary to Prussia

**May–July:** In response to French attacks on U.S. shipping to Britain, sends peace mission to France

### 1798

**March–April:** The Quasi-War begins with France; "XYZ Affair" made public
**May–June:** Proposes creation of the Department of the Navy
**July:** Signs the Alien and Sedition Acts

### 1799

**February:** Appoints a second peace mission to France

### 1800

**May:** Dismisses Secretary of War James McHenry and Secretary of State Timothy Pickering for their opposition to his peace policy with France
**September:** Endures public political criticism from Alexander Hamilton
**October:** Treaty ends the Quasi-War as well as the Franco-American alliance of 1778
**November 1:** Moves into the "President's House" (later called the White House), in the newly created capital city of Washington
**November 30:** Son Charles Adams dies in New York City
**December:** Defeated for reelection by Thomas Jefferson

### 1801

**January–February:** Makes so-called "midnight appointments" of Federalist judges, most importantly John Marshall as chief justice of the U.S. Supreme Court
**March 4:** As Jefferson is inaugurated, Adams retires to his farm in Quincy, Massachusetts

### 1802

**October 5:** Begins an autobiography, the work on which continues to 1807

### 1812

JANUARY: Resumes his long-suspended friendship and brilliant correspondence with Thomas Jefferson; letters are exchanged through 1826

### 1813

AUGUST 14: Daughter Abigail Adams Smith dies

### 1818

OCTOBER 28: Abigail Adams dies

### 1825

FEBRUARY 9: After an election too close to call, the House of Representatives names John Quincy Adams sixth president of the United States
MARCH 4: John Quincy Adams inaugurated

### 1826

JULY 4: John Adams dies, as does Thomas Jefferson

# Further Reading

Allison, John Murray. *Adams and Jefferson: The Story of a Friendship.* Norman: University of Oklahoma Press, 1966.

Bowen, Catherine Drinker. *John Adams and the American Revolution.* Boston: Little, Brown, 1950.

Brown, Ralph Adams. *The Presidency of John Adams.* Lawrence: University Press of Kansas, 1975.

Butterfield, L. H., ed. *Diary and Autobiography of John Adams.* Vols. 1–4. Cambridge, Mass.: Harvard University Press, 1961.

Butterfield, L. H., ed. *The Earliest Diary of John Adams.* Cambridge, Mass.: Harvard University Press, 1966.

Cappon, Lester J., ed. *The Adams-Jefferson Letters.* Chapel Hill: University of North Carolina Press, 1959.

Carey, George W. *The Political Writings of John Adams.* Washington, D.C.: Regnery, 2000.

Diggins, John Patrick, ed. *The Portable John Adams.* New York: Penguin, 2004.

Elkins, Stanley, and Eric McKitrick. *The Age of Federalism.* New York: Oxford University Press, 1993.

Ellis, Joseph J. *After the Revolution.* New York: Norton, 1979.

Ferling, John. *John Adams: A Life.* New York: Holt, 1992.

Howe, John R., Jr. *The Changing Political Thought of John Adams.* Princeton, N.J.: Princeton University Press, 1983.

Hutson, James H. *John Adams and the Diplomacy of the American Revolution.* Lexington: University Press of Kentucky, 1980.

Levin, Phyllis Lee. *Abigail Adams.* New York: St. Martin's, 1987.

McCullough, David. *John Adams.* New York: Simon and Schuster, 2001.

Peterson, Merrill D. *Adams and Jefferson: A Revolutionary Dialogue.* New York: Oxford University Press, 1960.

Sharp, James Roger. *American Politics in the Early Republic: The New Nation in Crisis.* New Haven, Conn.: Yale University Press, 1993.

Shaw, Peter. *The Character of John Adams.* Chapel Hill: University of North Carolina Press, 1976.

Shuffelton, Frank. *The Letters of John and Abigail Adams.* New York: Penguin, 2004.

Smith, Page. *John Adams.* Vols 1–2. Garden City, N.Y.: Doubleday, 1962.

Taylor, Robert J., ed. *Papers of John Adams.* Vols. 1–10. Cambridge, Mass.: Belknap Press of Harvard University Press, 1983.

# Index